UNDER  200 BY KNIT PICKS

Photography by Amy Cave

Printed in the United States of America

First Printing, 2016

ISBN 9781627671415

Versa Press, Inc
800-447-7829

www.versapress.com

CONTENTS

Astral Shawl	6	Leanan Hat	64
Favorite Buttoned Slippers	10	Lottie's Booties	68
Baltimore Hat	14	Autumn Arbor Hat	72
Broken Garter Cowl	18	Morana Mittens	76
Woven Garter Bag	22	Northern Shores Cowl	80
Dibona Cowl	26	Posie Bonnet	84
Sara Hat	30	Double Leaf Cowl	88
Giselle the Giraffe	34	Runner Hat	92
Happy Sheep Headband	40	Snowy Bunny	96
Heart Lace Mitts	44	Structured Slippers	100
Houndstooth Cowl	48	Voyageur Scarf	104
Kearsarge Shawl	52	Wave Mittens	108
Lazy Weekend Socks	56	Zigzagging Hat and Mitts	112
Daya Headband	60	Arri Hat	116

ASTRAL SHAWL

by Tian Connaughton

FINISHED MEASUREMENTS

About 66" wide at lower edge, 43" at upper edge, x 14" deep

YARN

Knit Picks Stroll Sock Yarn (75% Superwash Merino Wool, 25% Nylon; 231 yards/100g): Firecracker Heather 24587, 3 balls

NEEDLES

US 7 (4.5mm) 32" circular needles, or size to obtain gauge.
US 9 (5.5mm) 32" circular needles for CO, or size two sizes larger than used to obtain gauge

NOTIONS

Yarn Needle
Stitch Markers
Cable Needles (2)

GAUGE

17 sts and 31 rows = 4" in St st on smaller needles, blocked

Astral Shawl

Notes:

Astral is a crescent shaped shawl worked from the bottom up beginning with a lace edging. The lace edging flows into the stockinette body with an easy mesh transition. Short rows are worked in the stockinette section to shape the shawl. The shawl has 4 sts of Garter Stitch at each end, which is maintained throughout. Work RS chart rows (odd numbers) from right to left, and WS rows (even numbers) from left to right.

C2F: Sl 1 st on CN and hold to front, K1, K1 from CN.
C2B: Sl 1 st on CN and hold to back, K1, K1 from CN.
C3FB: Sl next st on CN and hold to front, Sl next st to 2nd CN and hold to back, K next st from left needle working in between front and back CN's, K1 from back CN, K1 from front CN.

Lace Pattern (worked flat)

Row 1 (RS): K4, SM, SKP, YO, C2F, *K1, C2B, YO, S2KP, YO, C2F; rep from * across to 5 sts before M, K1, C2B, YO, SKP, SM, K4.

Row 2, 4, 8, 10 (WS): K4, SM, P2, *K1, P3; rep from * across to 3 sts before M, K1, P2, SM, K4.

Row 3: K4, SM, SKP, YO, P1, *C3FB, P1, YO, S2KP, YO, P1; rep from * across to 6 sts before M, C3FB, P1, YO, SKP, SM, K4.

Row 5: K4, SM, SKP, *YO, C2B, K1, C2F, YO, S2KP; rep from * across to 7 sts before M, YO, C2B, K1, C2F, YO, SKP, SM, K4.

Row 6: K4, SM, P across to M, SM, K4.

Row 7: K4, SM, *K1, C2B, YO, S2KP, YO, C2F; rep from * across to 1 st before M, K1, SM, K4.

Row 9: K4, SM, C2F, *P1, YO, S2KP, YO, P1, C3FB; rep from * across to 7 sts before M, P1, YO, S2KP, YO, P1, C2F, SM, K4.

Row 11: K4, SM, *K1, C2F, YO, S2KP, YO, C2B; rep from * across to 1 st before M, K1, SM, K4.

Row 12: K4, SM, P across to M, SM, K4.

Rep Rows 1-12 for pattern.

DIRECTIONS

With larger needle, CO 297 sts.

Change to smaller needle.

Rows 1-3: Knit.

Row 4 (WS): K4, PM, K across to 4 sts before end of row, PM, K4.

Rows 5-52: Work 4 repeats of Lace Pattern.

Row 53 (RS): K4, SM, K1, *K2tog, K2; rep from * across to M, K4 – 225 sts remain.

Row 54 (WS): K4, SM, P across to M, SM, K4.

Row 55: K4, SM, K1, *K2tog, YO; rep from * across to M, K4.

Row 56: K4, SM, P across to M, SM, K4.

Row 57: K4, SM, K2, YO, S2KP, YO, *K1, YO, S2KP, YO; rep from * across to M, K4.

Row 58: K4, SM, P across to M, SM, K4.

Begin Short-row Shaping

Short-row 1 (RS): K117, turn.

Short-row 2 (WS): P9, turn.

Short-row 3: K8, SSK, K4, turn – 1 st dec.

Short-row 4: P12, P2tog, P4, turn – 1 st dec.

Short-row 5: K16, SSK, K4, turn – 1 st dec.

Short-row 6: P20, P2tog, P4, turn – 1 st dec.

Continue to work short-rows as established (working to 1 st before gap, SSK or P2tog, work next 4 sts, turn) until there are 4 sts before M on a WS row, turn – 185 sts remain.

Next Row (RS): K across to gap, SSK, K across to end of row – 184 sts remain.

Next Row (WS): K4, P across to gap, P2tog, P to last 4 sts, K4 – 183 sts remain.

Knit 4 rows, removing all M's.

Next Row: *K2tog, YO; rep from * across to 1 st before end of row, K1.

BO Row (WS): *K2tog, return st to left hand needle; rep from * to end. Break yarn and pull through remaining loop. All stitches bound off.

Finishing

Weave in all ends. Block to measurements.

Astral Chart

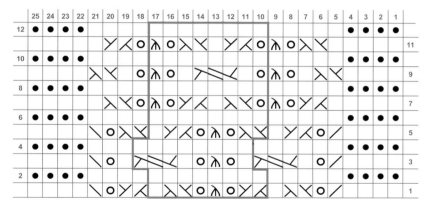

Legend

knit
RS: knit stitch
WS: purl stitch

k2tog
Knit two stitches together as one stitch
WS: Purl 2 stitches together

YO
yarn over

C2F
Sl 1 st on CN, hold in front. K1, K1 from CN

C2B
Sl 1 st on CN, hold in back. K1, K1 from CN

sl2k1P
Sl 2 sts, K1, pass slipped sts over knit st

purl
RS: purl stitch
WS: knit stitch

——— **pattern repeat**

SSK
Slip one stitch as if to knit, slip another stitch as if to knit. Insert left-hand needle into front of these 2 stitches and knit them together

C3FB
Sl next st to CN, hold in front. Sl next st to CN, hold in back. Knit next st from left needle working inbetween front and back CN, K1 from back CN, K1 from front CN

FAVORITE BUTTONED SLIPPERS

by Faye Kennington

FINISHED MEASUREMENTS

6.75 (7.5, 8.5)" foot circumference x 8.5 (9.5, 10.5)" foot length; to be worn with approximately .5" negative ease

YARN

Knit Picks Swish DK (100% Superwash Merino Wool; 123 yards/50g): Marine Heather 24949, 1 (2, 2) balls

NEEDLES

US 6 (4mm) DPNs or two 24" circular needles for two circulars technique, or one 32" or longer circular needle for Magic Loop technique, or size to obtain gauge

NOTIONS

Yarn Needle
Two Stitch Markers
Two 0.5" Buttons

GAUGE

21 sts and 28 rows = 4" in stranded St st in the round, blocked

Favorite Buttoned Slippers

Notes:

These asymmetrical DK weight slippers have a selvedge slit on the outside of the edge of the upper arch that is closed by a favorite button at the ankle. They're lightweight slippers or bed socks and a small easy project for you or your guests to use around the house.

The slippers' heels turn with short rows made by shadow wrapping. With this technique, a second "twin" stitch is created from a stitch in the previous row to match the stitch in the current row at the point of the short row turn. On the next row, when it comes to working over the twinned stitches, they are treated as one stitch, either knit or purled together depending on the side of the work. Shadow wraps are easy to do, do not leave any holes in the work and lend a neat appearance to the finished piece.

For a video tutorial of Judy's Magic Cast On, see http://tutorials.knitpicks.com/wptutorials/judys-magic-cast-on/

M1: Increase 1 st using a backwards loop cast on.

KYOK: K, YO, K in one st. 2 sts inc.

Knit Twinned Stitch (TWK): Knit into the st directly below next stitch on left needle and place the new st beside the stitch on the current row to create a twinned stitch - 2 sts from 1 st.

Purl Twinned Stitch (TWP): WYIF, Sl 1 st P-wise to right needle, insert the left needle tip into the st below the slipped st on the right needle lifting the front leg, purl into this st with the right needle, then slip both sts of twin st from right needle to left needle without twisting - 2 sts from 1 st

DIRECTIONS

The slippers are worked from the toe up, in the round until the work is split to create the asymmetrical slit that is buttoned at the heel. Make two; 1 left and 1 right.

Toe

Using Judy's Magic Cast On, CO 18 (20, 22) sts divided evenly over 2 needles. Commence working in the round; divide work over 3 or 4 DPNs if desired.
Rnds 1 and 3: Knit.
Rnd 2: *PM, K1, M1, K7 (8, 9), M1, K1; rep from * twice – 22 (24, 26) sts. SMs as they come.
Rnd 4: *K1, M1, K to last st before M, M1, K1; rep from * twice – inc 4 sts.
Work Rnds 3 & 4 two (three, three) more times – 34 (40, 42) sts.

Sizes 6.75 & 8.5" Only: K 1 rnd. Next Rnd: K18 (0, 22), M1, K to last st, M1, K1 – 36 (40, 44) sts.

All Sizes: Knit in the round until work measures 2.75 (3, 3.5)" long.

Split

In this section, the split is created. Note the differing instructions for left and right slippers. After this section, work in the round will cease and flat work will begin. This may be most comfortable on a circular needle, but can be managed over 2 DPNs. Do not remove markers.

Left Slipper

Next Rnd: K5 (6, 6), KYOK twice, K to end of rnd – 40 (44, 48) sts.
Next Row: K8 (9, 9), turn to commence working flat as new start of row.

Right Slipper

Next Rnd: K10 (12, 13), KYOK twice, K to end of rnd – 40 (44, 48) sts.
Next Row (RS): K13 (15, 16), turn to commence working flat as new start of row.

Both Slippers

Row 1 (WS): WYIF Sl 3, P to end.
Row 2 (RS): WYIB Sl 3, K to end.
Work these 2 rows until slippers measure 6.5 (7.5, 8.25)" long, or are 2 (2, 2.25)" shorter than desired finished length.

Heel Flap

Heel Flap will be worked over the middle sts between the 2 Ms.
Row 1 (WS): WYIF Sl 3, P to 1 st before 2nd M, TWP.
Row 2 (RS): K to 1 st before M, TWK.
Row 3: P to 1 st before TWP st in previous WS row, TWP.
Row 4: K to 1 st before TWK st in previous RS row, TWK.
Work Rows 3 & 4 five (five, six) more times – 7 (7, 8) twinned sts on each side of center 5 (6, 7) sts.

Now begin working sts beyond M again to join heel to rest of slipper.
Row 5 (WS): P to M working all twinned sts as one, SM, TWP.
Row 6 (RS): K to M working all twinned sts as one, TWK.
Row 7: P to twinned st in previous WS row, work all twinned st as one, TWP.
Row 8: K to twinned st in previous WS row, work all twinned st as one, TWK.
Work Rows 7 & 8 four (five, six) more times.

I-Cord Edging

Left Slipper

Work all twinned sts as one. Remove Ms as you come to them.
Set Up: Without turning, K to end of row.
Next Row: *P2, Sl 1, P1, PSSO, transfer last 3 sts from right-hand needle to the left; rep from * until 3 sts remain.
Next 4 Rows: P3, transfer last 3 sts from right-hand needle to the left. Work this row 3 more times or more until half the length of the cord is the right length for a strap over the ankle and buttonhole.
Next Row: P3tog.

Right Slipper

Work all twinned sts as one. Remove Ms as you come to them. Cut yarn and recommence on RS of other end of work.
Next Row: *K2, Sl 1, K1, PSSO, transfer last 3 sts from right-hand needle to the left; rep from * until 3 sts remain.
Next 4 Rows: K3, transfer last 3 sts from right-hand needle to the left. Work this row 3 more times or more until half the length of the cord is the right length for a strap over the ankle and buttonhole.
Next Row: K3tog.

Both Slippers

Cut yarn leaving 6" tail, pass tail through last st. Fold last 5 rows so that the end meets the top corner of the slipper to form a button hole loop. Sew in place.

Finishing

Block to measurements. Sew button on top of slit opposite the iCord loop. Weave in loose ends.

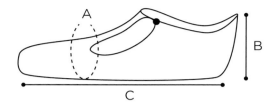

A 6.75 (7.5, 8.5)"
B 2 (2.5, 2.75)"
C 8.5 (9.5, 10.5)"

BALTIMORE HAT

by Megan Nodecker

FINISHED MEASUREMENTS

13.25 (16.75, 20, 23.25)" around x 6 (7.5, 9.75, 10.75)" tall with brim folded.
To fit: Baby (12-14"), Child (15-18"), Adult Small (19-22"), Adult Large (23+")

YARN

Knit Picks Biggo Yarn (50% Superwash Merino Wool, 50% Nylon; 110 yards/100g): Dove Heather 25615, 1 (1, 2, 3) hanks

NEEDLES

US 10.75 (7mm) 16" circular needles plus DPNs, or size to obtain gauge

NOTIONS

Yarn Needle
Stitch Marker
Pompom Maker (optional)

GAUGE

12 sts and 18 rows = 4" in Body Pattern, blocked

Baltimore Hat

Notes:

This hat is knit in the round from the bottom up. It has an extra-long brim to be folded double once complete. The body can be knit using either the charted or written directions and really shines once it's been blocked. The crown uses single and double decreases to create a seamless transition. An optional pom pom can be added to the top. If working the chart, read each row from right to left, as a RS row.

Single Rib (worked in the round over an even number of sts)
All Rnds: *K1, P1, rep from * to end of rnd.

Body Pattern (worked in the round over multiples of 10 sts)
Rnd 1, 2, 3: *K7, P3, rep from * to end of rnd.
Rnd 4: *P1, K5, P1, K3, rep from * to end of rnd.
Rnd 5: K1, *P1, K3, P1, K5, rep from * to last 9 sts, P1, K3, P1, K4.
Rnd 6, 7, 8: K2, *P3, K7, rep from * to last 8 sts, P3, K5.
Rnd 9: K1, *P1, K3, P1, K5, rep from * to last 9 sts, P1, K3, P1, K4.
Rnd 10: *P1, K5, P1, K3, rep from * to end of rnd.
Rep Rnds 1-10 for pattern

Centered Double Decrease (S2KP2):
Sl 2 sts as if to K them together, K 1 st then pass the 2 slipped sts over the K st.

DIRECTIONS
Brim
Loosely CO 40 (50, 60, 70) sts, PM and join in the round, being careful not to twist sts.

Work in Single Rib for 4 (5, 6, 6)".

Body
Sizes 13.25 (20)" ONLY: Work Body Pattern Chart or Body Pattern written instructions 1 (2) time(s).

Sizes 16.75 (23.25)" ONLY: Work Rnds 6-10 of Body Pattern Chart or Body Pattern written instructions. Then, work Rnds 1-10 1 (2) more time(s).

Crown Decreases
Rnd 1: *K7, P1, P2TOG, rep from * to end of rnd. 36 (45, 54, 63) sts.
Rnd 2: *K7, P2, rep from * to end of rnd.
Rnd 3: *K7, P2TOG, rep from * to end of rnd. 32 (40, 48, 56) sts.
Rnd 4: *K7, P1, rep from * to end of rnd.
Rnd 5: *K2, S2KP2, K2, P1, rep from * to end of rnd. 24 (30, 36, 42) sts.
Rnd 6: *K5, P1, rep from * to end of rnd.
Rnd 7: *K1, S2KP2, K1, P1, rep from * to end of rnd. 16 (20, 24, 28) sts.
Rnd 8: *K3, P1, rep from * to end of rnd.

Sizes 13.25 (16.75)" ONLY: Cut yarn and thread through remaining sts, pull snug and secure.

Rnd 9: *S2KP2, P1, rep from * to end of rnd. - (-. 12, 14) sts
Rnd 10: *K1, P1, rep from * to end of rnd.

Cut yarn and thread through remaining sts, pull snug and secure.

Finishing
Weave in ends, block and add pompom.

Body Pattern Chart

10	9	8	7	6	5	4	3	2	1	
			●						●	10
				●				●		9
					●	●	●			8
					●	●	●			7
					●	●	●			6
				●				●		5
			●						●	4
●	●	●								3
●	●	●								2
●	●	●								1

Legend

☐ **knit**
knit stitch

⊡ **purl**
purl stitch

BROKEN GARTER COWL

by Sarah Sundermeyer

FINISHED MEASUREMENTS
23 (46)" circumference x 8 (10)" high

YARN
Knit Picks Preciosa Tonal Worsted
(100% Merino Wool; 273 yards/100g):
Boysenberry 26728, 1 (2) balls

NEEDLES
US 9 (5.5mm) 16 (32)" circular needles, or
size to obtain gauge

NOTIONS
Yarn Needle
Stitch Marker

GAUGE
19 sts and 32 rows = 4" in Broken Garter
Stitch Pattern, blocked. (Gauge for this
project is approximate)

Broken Garter Cowl

Notes:

This cowl is knit in the round on circular needles, using only knit and purl stitches. The stitch pattern can be worked from either the written directions or the chart.

Broken Garter Stitch Pattern (in the round, over multiples of 4 sts)

Rounds 1,3,5,7: K all sts.
Round 2: *K1, P3, rep from * to end of rnd.
Round 4: Rep Rnd 2.
Round 6: *P2, K1, P1, rep from * to end of rnd.
Round 8: Rep Rnd 6.
Rep Rnds 1-8 for pattern.

DIRECTIONS

CO 108 (216) sts. PM and join in the round, being careful not to twist your stitches.

Repeat Rnds 1-8 of the Broken Garter Stitch Pattern or Chart 8 (10) times, or until desired height.

Final Rnd: K all sts.

BO all sts.

Finishing

Weave in ends, wash and block to finished measurements.

Broken Garter Chart

4	3	2	1	
●		●	●	8
				7
●		●	●	6
				5
●	●	●		4
				3
●	●	●		2
				1

Legend

□ **knit** knit stitch

▣ **purl** purl stitch

WOVEN GARTER BAG

by Sherrie Kibler

FINISHED MEASUREMENTS
7.5" wide x 9" high; 45" long shoulder strap

YARN
Knit Picks Wool of the Andes Worsted (100% Peruvian Highland Wool; 110 yards/50g): MC Icicle Heather 25992, 2 skeins; C1 Midnight Heather 25640, C2 Dove Heather 24077; 1 skein each

NEEDLES
US 8 (5mm) straight or circular needles, or size to obtain gauge
US 6 (4mm) DPNs, or two sizes smaller than needle to obtain gauge

NOTIONS
Yarn Needle
Size F Crochet hook (optional)
1" button

GAUGE
16 sts and 30 rows = 4" in Garter stitch on larger needles, blocked

Woven Garter Bag

Notes:

Color swapping between the main color background and two contrast colors results in the fabric of this bag taking on a woven look when viewed from the reverse side.

Worked flat as one continuous piece, the bag is folded and stitched along the sides, then trimmed with a knit-on I-cord. If a reversible bag is desired, the I-cord trim may be continued onto the inside of the bag.

Yarn Color Swapping

The striped pattern is created by swapping yarn colors every two rows. Carry the idle yarns loosely along the edge so that the needed color is available when needed.

I-cord

CO 4 sts onto a DPN (leave an 8" tail for stitching). *K4. Slide the sts to the right end of the needle. Rep from * until the I-cord is the desired length.

Knit-on I-cord

Step 1: K4.

Step 2: Use a crochet hook or the tip of your knitting needle to create a 5th st by pulling the working yarn up the through the edge of the knitted fabric. Put the newly created st on the right needle.

Step 3: Slide the 5 sts to the right end of the needle.

Step 4: K3, then K2tog TBL.

Repeat Steps 1-4 along the piece edge, taking care to space your picked-up 5th sts closely along the edge to avoid puckering.

DIRECTIONS

CO 30 sts using a knitted CO with MC and larger needles.

Row 1 (WS): With MC, K all sts.

Row 2 (RS): With MC, WYIF Sl 1 P-wise, K all sts until last st, WYIF Sl 1 P-wise.

Row 3: With C1, K all sts.

Row 4: With C1, WYIF Sl 1 P-wise, K all sts until last st, WYIF Sl 1 P-wise.

Row 5: With C2, K all sts.

Row 6: With C2, WYIF Sl 1 P-wise, K all sts until last st, WYIF Sl 1 P-wise.

Repeat Rows 1-6 until the piece measures 18" from CO edge, ending on an odd row.

Flap

Continue alternating colors as you continue the six row repeats, but dec1 st on each edge of the piece on all even rows as follows until 4 sts remain:

Rows 1, 3, 5: Using respective yarn color, K all sts.

Rows 2, 4, 6: Using respective yarn color, K2tog, K all sts until the last 2 sts, K2tog. 2 sts dec.

When 4 sts remain, BO all sts.

Finishing

Weave in ends; wash and block to diagram dimensions.

Seaming

Fold the piece from CO edge to the beginning of flap decreases so that the wrong sides of fabric are facing each other on the inside of the piece. Note that the desired exterior of the fabric (RS) is on the outside. Align stripe colors and pin in place. Use an overcast stitch and I-cord trim yarn color to seam both sides of piece along the edge, catching the outside loop of the slipped edge sts as you work. Take care to run your seam closely along the edge so that it is covered by the Knit-on I-cord trim.

I-cord Seam Trim

To create the strap loops on either side of the bag, use MC to create a 3" I-cord (see Notes). Keep the 4 sts live on DPN.

Starting at the top of the side seam on the outside of the bag, begin working a Knit-on I-cord (see Notes). Work the Knit-on I-cord down the first side seam, across the bottom, and up the second side seam. Take care to space your picked up sts closely along the seam edge to avoid puckering at the seam.

When you reach the top edge of the bag, stop picking up sts and continue to work 3" of unattached I-cord as was done on the opposite side of the bag. Do not stitch the end of the I-cord trim to the bag at this time. If a reversible bag is desired, return to working Knit-on I-cord along the inside edge of the bag. BO I-cord sts.

I-cord Flap Trim

The trim on the flap edge is worked as flat St st at the beginning and end, and is worked as a Knit-on I-cord in between.

With MC, CO 4 sts onto a DPN. (Leave an 8" tail for stitching.)

Row 1: K all sts.

Row 2: P all sts.

Repeat Rows 1-2 once more.

With 4 sts on the DPN and the right side of the flap facing, begin working Knit-on I-cord along the flap edge, starting about .5" from the beginning of the flap. When you reach the center point of the flap, stop picking up sts for the I-cord and create a 4-stitch unattached 3" length of I-cord.

Resume the Knit-on I-cord at the center point where you stopped picking up the sts. Continue the Knit-on I-cord until you are .5" from the end of the flap. Work 4 rows in St st as was done at the beginning of the flap trim, then BO leaving an 8" tail.

I-cord Strap

With MC, CO 4 sts onto a DPN. Work a 100" I-cord. Graft the ends of the I-cord together to form one continuous loop. If you created a reversible bag and the I-cord trim loops at the top of the bag are already closed, leave the I-cord strap ends free, and close the strap loop as a final step.

Fold the loop in half to form a double stranded strap about 50" long. Tie a double-stranded knot about 1" from both ends of the strap; one of the knots should incorporate the graft so it is not visible.

Slip one strap loop through the loose seam I-cord trim at the top edge of the bag. Stitch the I-cord trim to the inside of the bag.

Twist the strap to the desired tightness and length. Slip the free end of the strap through the second I-cord trim at the top of the bag; stitch the I-cord trim in place inside the bag.

Final Details

Wrap the flat ends of the I-cord trim around the ends of the flap. Stitch in place. Twist the loop at the center point of the flap and stitch on the underside. Weave in any remaining ends. If desired, pin and lightly steam block completed bag, focusing on smoothing I-cord trim.

Close the flap to determine button location. Sew a 1" button onto bag body.

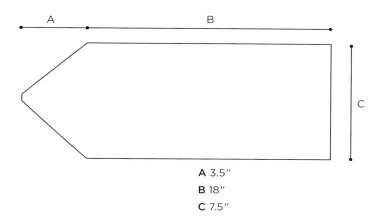

A 3.5″
B 18″
C 7.5″

DIBONA COWL

by Joyce Fassbender

FINISHED MEASUREMENTS
23.5" circumference x 10" depth, blocked

YARN
Knit Picks Gloss Fingering (70% Merino Wool, 30% Silk; 220 yards/50g): MC Navy 27018, C1 Robot 25015; 1 skein each

NEEDLES
US 4 (3.5mm) 16" circular needle, or size to obtain gauge

NOTIONS
Yarn Needle
Stitch Markers

GAUGE
24 sts and 32 rows = 4" in St st, blocked.
29 sts and 32 rows = 4" over Chart 1 worked in the rnd, blocked

Dibona Cowl

Notes:

The cowl pattern is worked in the round. The complexity of the appearance of the stripe pattern is an illusion caused by the arrangement of the yarn overs and decreases in the lace. The stripes are worked straight across each row. The pattern is charted.

In order to increase the depth of the cowl, work additional repeats of Rnds 1-20 of Chart 1. Each additional repeat will add 2.5" to the depth.

In order to increase the circumference of the cowl, work additional repeats of chart per round. Thirty-four additional stitches will need to be cast on per round for each added repeat. Each additional repeat adds 4.75" in circumference.

Work all charted rows from right to left.

Use stitch markers at beginning of round and between pattern repeats if necessary.

DIRECTIONS

Cast on 170 stitches with MC using Long Tail cast on. Place marker and join in the rnd taking care not to twist.

Set Up Rnds

Rnd 1: P all sts.
Rnd 2: K all sts.
Rnd 3: P all sts.

Begin working chart.

Work Chart

Work Rnds 1-20 of Chart 1 three times over length of neck warmer. The chart is repeated five (5) times per rnd. Change color as indicated on the chart.

Work Rnds 1 – 13 of Chart 1 once. Break C1.

End Rnds

Rnd 1: P all sts.
Rnd 2: K all sts.
Rnd 3: P all sts.

Finishing

Loosely bind off all sts. Weave in ends, wash and lay flat to dry.

Chart 1

Legend:
- **knit** — knit stitch (empty square)
- **O** — yo — yarn over
- **⋏ (sl1 k2tog psso)** — slip 1, k2tog, pass slip stitch over k2tog
- **╱ (k3tog)** — knit three stitches together as one
- **▲ (sl2 k3tog p2sso)** — slip 2 stitches, k3tog, pass 2 slipped stitches over k3tog
- **▓ (CC)** — contrast color

34	33	32	31	30	29	28	27	26	25	24	23	22	21	20	19	18	17	16	15	14	13	12	11	10	9	8	7	6	5	4	3	2	1	Rnd
O																																O		20
O																				O	⋏	O										O		19
																																		18
O																O		⋏				O									O		17
																																		16
O (CC)															O					⋏				O							O		15
																																		14
O									O							╱		⋏					O							O		13
																																		12
O										O						╱					▲				O					O		11
																																		10
O								O	▲	O																					O		9
																																		8
O					O			▲		O																				O		7
																																		6
O (CC)			O				▲				O																		O		5
																																		4
O	O			╱		⋏			O																	O		3
																																		2
O	O					╱						▲					O									O		1

SARA HAT

by Trelly Hernández

FINISHED MEASUREMENTS

16" ribbing circumference x 8" high

YARN

Knit Picks Brava Bulky (100% Premium Acrylic; 136 yards/100g): Wine 25731, 1 ball

NEEDLES

US 7 (4.5mm) 16" circular needles, or size to obtain gauge
US 9 (5.5mm) 16" circular needles plus DPN's, or 2 sizes larger than needle to obtain gauge

NOTIONS

Yarn Needle
Stitch Marker

GAUGE

20 sts and 24 rows = 4" in Ribbing Pattern with smaller needles, lightly blocked

Sara Hat

Notes:

This hat is worked in the round, with an attractive ribbing pattern and an easy lace pattern that is charted. Repeat each row of the Sara Chart pattern 8 times each round, reading chart rows from right to left.

Left Twist (LT): Skip 1 st on left needle, K 2nd st TBL and leave on needle, K the skipped st, then drop both original sts from left needle.

Right Twist (RT): Skip 1 st on left needle, K 2nd st and leave on needle, K the skipped st, then drop both original sts from left needle.

Sl1-k1-psso: Sl 1 st, K1, PSSO. 1 st dec.
Sl1-k2tog-psso: Sl 1 st, K2tog, PSSO. 2 sts dec.

Ribbing Pattern (worked in the round over multiples of 5 sts)
Rnd 1: *K1, LT, P2, repeat from * to end.
Rnd 2: *RT, K1, P2, repeat from * to end.
Rep Rnds 1-2 for pattern.

DIRECTIONS

With smaller needles and using Long Tail Cast-On, CO 80 sts, place marker and join in the round being careful not to twist your sts.
Work Ribbing Pattern 6 times in total.
Switch to bigger needles and work Sara Chart twice.

Crown

Switch to DPN's as needed.
Rnd 1: *K2tog, K3, repeat from * to end. 64 sts.
Rnd 2: K.
Rnd 3: *K2tog, K2, repeat from * to end. 48 sts.
Rnd 4: K.
Rnd 5: *K2tog, K1, repeat from * to end. 32 sts.
Rnd 6: K.
Rnd 7: *K2tog, repeat from * to end. 16 sts.
Rnd 8: K.

Finishing

Break the yarn leaving a long tail, and with the yarn needle pass the tail through the remaining sts, pull tight. Weave in ends. Block lightly.

Sara Chart

10	9	8	7	6	5	4	3	2	1	
										14
			O	入	O					13
										12
		O		入		O				11
										10
	O			入			O			9
										8
O				入				O		7
										6
O	λ						/	O		5
										4
O	λ						/	O		3
										2
O	λ						/	O		1

Legend

knit
knit stitch

yo
Yarn Over

k2tog
Knit two stitches together as one stitch

sl1 k psso
slip 1, knit 1, pass slipped stitch over knit 1

sl1 k2tog psso
slip 1, k2tog, pass slip stitch over k2tog

GISELLE THE GIRAFFE

by Stana D. Sortor

FINISHED MEASUREMENTS
13" tall standing, 9" tall sitting

YARN
Knit Picks Palette (100% Peruvian Highland Wool; 231 yards/50g): MC Cornmeal 24252, C1 Masala 24248, C2 Bark 23737; 1 ball each

NEEDLE
US 3 (3.25mm) DPNs or two 24" circular needles for two circulars technique, or one 32" or longer circular needle for Magic Loop technique, or size to obtain gauge

NOTIONS
Yarn Needle
Stitch Markers
Polyester fiberfill
2 - 8 mm Safety Eyes (optional) or Scrap Yarn

GAUGE
28 sts and 34 rows = 4" in St st in the round, blocked

Giselle the Giraffe

Notes:

The baby giraffe is knit in the round. The body and neck is knit in one piece. The head, legs, tail, ears and horns are knit separately and sewn on.

All charts are followed from bottom to top, working each row from right to left. Repeat Giraffe Chart 1 three times across the round, Giraffe Chart 2 six times across the round, Giraffe Chart 3 three times across the round, and Giraffe Chart 4 two times across the round.

Giraffe Chart 1
Round 1: K1 in MC, K2 in C1, K3 in MC, K3 in C1, K1 in MC.
Round 2: KFB in MC, (K2 in C1, K1 in MC) 3 times.
Round 3: K2 in C1, K2 in MC, K4 in C1, K2 in MC, K1 in C1.
Round 4: KFB in C1, K1 in MC, K1 in C1, (K2 in MC, K2 in C1) twice.
Round 5: K1 in C1, K1 in MC, K3 in C1, K3 in MC, K2 in C1, K2 in MC.
Round 6: KFB in MC, K3 in C1, K2 in MC, K1 in C1, K1 in MC, K3 in C1, K1 in MC.
Round 7: K1 in C1, K2 in MC, K1 in C1, K1 in MC, K2 in C1, K1 in MC, K3 in C1, K2 in MC.
Round 8: KFB in C1, K3 in MC, K2 in C1, K4 in MC, K2 in C1, K1 in MC.
Round 9: K3 in C1, K2 in MC, K1 in C1, K2 in MC, K2 in C1, K3 in MC, K1 in C1.
Round 10: K2 in C1, K1 in MC, K1 in C1, K3 in MC, K4 in C1, K2 in MC, K1 in C1.
Round 11: K2 in MC, K4 in C1, K1 in MC, K5 in C1, K2 in MC.
Round 12: K2 in MC, K3 in C1, K2 in MC, K3 in C1, K2 in MC, K1 in C1, K1 in MC.
Round 13: K1 in MC, K3 in C1, K3 in MC, K1 in C1, K3 in MC, K3 in C1.
Round 14: K4 in MC, K2 in C1, K3 in MC, K1 in C1, K1 in MC, K3 in C1.
Round 15: SSK in MC, K1 in MC, K4 in C1, K1 in MC, K4 in C1, K2 in MC.
Round 16: SSK in MC, K4 in C1, K2 in MC, K2 in C1, K3 in MC.
Round 17: SSK in MC, K3 in MC, K1 in C1, K3 in MC, K2 in C1, K1 in MC.
Round 18: SSK in MC, K1 in MC, K3 in C1, K2 in MC, K3 in C1.
Round 19: SSK in MC, K2 in C1, K3 in MC, K2 in C1, K1 in MC.
Round 20: SSK in MC, K7 in MC.

Giraffe Chart 2
Round 1: K2 in MC, K2 in C1.
Round 2: KFB in MC, K1 in MC, KFB in C1, K1 in C1.
Round 3: K1 in MC, K1 in C1, K4 in MC.
Round 4: KFB in C1, K1 in C1, K1 in MC, KFB in MC, K2 in MC.
Round 5: K4 in C1, K4 in MC.
Round 6: (KFB in MC, K2 in C1, K1 in MC) 2 times.
Round 7: K6 in MC, K4 in C1.
Round 8: K2 in MC, K1 in C1, K3 in MC, K4 in C1.
Round 9: K1 in MC, K3 in C1, K3 in MC, K1 in C1, K2 in MC.
Round 10: K2 in MC, K2 in C1, K6 in MC.
Round 11: K2 in MC, K4 in C1, K2 in MC, K1 in C1, K1 in MC.
Round 12: K3 in MC, K2 in C1, K2 in MC, K3 in C1.
Round 13: K1 in C1, K6 in MC, K3 in C1.
Round 14: K2 in MC, K2 in C1, K3 in MC, K2 in C1, K1 in MC.
Round 15: K1 in MC, K4 in C1, K5 in MC.

Round 16: K5 in C1, K5 in MC.
Round 17: K1 in MC, K3 in C1, K3 in MC, K2 in C1, K1 in MC.
Round 18: K6 in MC, K4 in C1.
Round 19: K2 in MC, K1 in C1, K2 in MC, K4 in C1, K1 in MC.
Round 20: K1 in MC, K3 in C1, K2 in MC, K2 in C1, K2 in MC.
Round 21: K5 in C1, K5 in MC.
Round 22: SSK in C1, K1 in C1, K3 in MC, K1 in C1, K3 in MC.
Round 23: K1 in MC, (K2 in C1, K2 in MC) twice.
Round 24: SSK in MC, K2 in MC, K4 in C1, K1 in MC.
Round 25: K4 in MC, K4 in C1.
Round 26: SSK in MC, K2 in MC, K3 in C1, K1 in MC.
Round 27: K2 in C1, K2 in MC, K1 in C1, K2 in MC.
Round 28: SSK in C1, K1 in C1, K4 in MC.
Round 29: K1 in C1, K4 in MC, K1 in C1.
Round 30: SSK in MC, K2 in MC, K2 in C1.
Round 31: K4 in MC, K1 in C1.
Round 32: K5 in MC.

Giraffe Chart 3
Round 1: K2 in MC, K2 in C1, K3 in MC, K1 in C1, K2 in MC.
Round 2: K1 in MC, K3 in C1, K2 in MC, K3 in C1, K1 in MC.
Round 3: K1 in MC, K4 in C1, K1 in MC, K2 in C1, K2 in MC.
Round 4: K1 in C1, K2 in MC, K2 in C1, K5 in MC.
Round 5: K2 in C1, K7 in MC, K1 in C1.
Round 6: K1 in C1, K1 in MC, (K2 in MC, K2 in C1) twice.
Round 7: K4 in MC, K3 in C1, K2 in MC, K1 in C1.
Round 8: SSK in MC, K2 in MC, K4 in C1, K2 in MC.
Round 9: K2 in MC, K4 in C1, K3 in MC.
Round 10: K3 in MC, K2 in C1, K4 in MC.
Round 11: K1 in C1, K3 in MC, K2 in C1, K3 in MC.
Round 12: K2 in C1, K6 in MC, K1 in C1.
Round 13: K2 in C1, K5 in MC, K2 in C1, K2 in MC.
Round 14: (K1 in C1, K3 in MC) twice, K1 in C1.
Round 15: K1 in C1, K2 in MC, K3 in C1, K3 in MC.
Round 16: SSK in MC, K2 in MC, K3 in C1, K2 in MC.
Round 17: K2 in MC, K3 in C1, K3 in MC.
Round 18: K3 in MC, K1 in C1, K2 in MC, K1 in C1, K1 in MC.
Round 19: K6 in MC, K2 in C1.
Round 20: K1 in C1, K2 in MC, K1 in C1, K3 in MC, K1 in C1.
Round 21: K2 in MC, K3 in C1, K3 in MC.
Round 22: K3 in MC, K3 in C1, K2 in MC.
Round 23: K3 in MC, K2 in C1, K3 in MC.
Round 24: SSK in MC, K6 in MC.

Giraffe Chart 4
Round 1: K2 in MC, K2 in C1, K3 in MC, K2 in C1, K1 in MC.
Round 2: K1 in MC, K4 in C1, K3 in MC, K1 in C1, K1 in MC.
Round 3: K2 in MC, K2 in C1, K3 in MC, K2 in C1, K1 in MC.
Round 4: K6 in MC, K4 in C1.
Round 5: K1 in MC, K2 in C1, K3 in MC, K4 in C1.
Round 6: K4 in C1, K6 in MC.
Round 7: K1 in MC, K2 in C1, K3 in MC, K2 in C1, K2 in C1.
Round 8: K5 in MC, K4 in C1, K1 in MC.
Round 9: K1 in MC, K2 in C1, K2 in MC, K4 in C1, K1 in MC.
Round 10: K2 in MC, K1 in C1, K3 in MC, K2 in C1, K2 in MC.

I-Cord (worked over 3 sts)
All Rows: *K3, slide sts to other end of DPN pulling yarn firmly; rep from *, creating a tube., K3.

DIRECTIONS
Head
Using DPNs, with MC CO 4 sts and divide evenly on 3 needles, leaving a long tail. PM, being careful not to twist sts, join to begin working in the round.

Round 1: Knit.
Round 2: KFB all around. 8 sts.
Round 3: Knit.
Round 4: *KFB, K1; repeat from * around. 12 sts.
Round 5: Knit.
Round 6: *KFB, K1; repeat from * around. 18 sts.
Round 7: Knit.
Round 8: *KFB, K2; repeat from * around. 24 sts.
Round 9: Knit.
Round 10: *KFB, K3; repeat from * around. 30 sts.
Rounds 11 - 30: Work Giraffe Chart 1, repeating Giraffe Chart 1 three times per round. 24 sts. After completing the chart, thread the tail of yarn from the CO sts onto a yarn needle. Stitch through all of the CO sts, pull up tight to close the hole, and stitch to secure. Stuff the head with fiberfill. Apply the safety eyes if using them.
Round 31: SSK all around, 12 sts.

Finish stuffing the head. Cut the yarn, thread the tail of yarn onto a yarn needle. Pull tail through all of the sts on DPNs, pull up tight to close the hole, and stitch to secure.

Body
Using DPNs, with MC CO 6 sts and divide evenly on 3 needles, leaving a long tail. PM, being careful not to twist sts, join to begin working in the round.

Round 1: Knit.
Round 2: KFB all around, 12 sts.
Round 3: Knit.
Round 4: KFB all around, 24 sts.
Rounds 5 - 36: Work Giraffe Chart 2, repeating Giraffe Chart 2 six times per round. 30 sts. After completing the chart, thread the tail of yarn from the CO sts onto a yarn needle. Pull tail through all of the CO sts, pull up tight to close the hole, and stitch to secure. Stuff the body with fiberfill. Continue with neck.
Rounds 37 - 60: Work Giraffe Chart 3, repeating Giraffe Chart 3 three times per round. 21 sts.

BO. Leave a long tail of yarn. Finish stuffing the neck.

Legs (make 4)
Using DPNs, with MC CO 20 sts and divide evenly on 3 needles, leaving a long tail. PM, being careful not to twist sts, join to begin working in the round.

Round 1: Knit.
Rounds 2 - 11: Work Giraffe Chart 4, repeating Giraffe Chart 4 two times per round. Cut off C1.
Rounds 12 – 25: Knit. Cut off MC. Attach C2.
Round 26: Knit. Stuff the leg with fiberfill.
Round 27: *KFB, K1; repeat from * around. 30 sts.
Rounds 28 - 32: Knit.
Round 33: *SSK, K1; repeat from * around. 20 sts.
Round 34: Knit.
Round 35: SSK all around. 10 sts.

Finish stuffing the leg. Cut the yarn, thread the tail of yarn onto a yarn needle. Pull tail through all of the sts on DPNs, pull up tight to close the hole, and stitch to secure.

Ears (make 2)
Using DPNs, with MC CO 8 sts and divide evenly on 2 needles, leaving a long tail. PM, being careful not to twist sts, join to begin working in the round.

Round 1: Knit.
Round 2: *KFB, K3; repeat from * around. 10 sts.
Round 3: *KFB, K4; repeat from * around. 12 sts.
Rounds 4 -& 5: Knit.
Round 6: *SSK, K4; repeat from * around. 10 sts.
Round 7: *SSK, K3; repeat from * around. 8 sts.
Round 8: *SSK, K2; repeat from * around. 6 sts.
Round 9: *SSK, K1; repeat from * around. 4 sts.

Cut the yarn, thread the tail of yarn onto a yarn needle. Pull tail through all of the sts on DPNs, pull up tight to close the hole, and stitch to secure.

Horns (make 2)
Using DPNs, with C1 CO 3 sts onto one DPN. Work I-cord for 5 rounds. Cut the yarn, thread the tail of yarn onto a yarn needle. Pull tail through all of the sts on DPNs, pull up tight to close the hole, and stitch to secure.

Tail
With MC CO 3 sts onto one DPN. Work I-cord for 2". BO. Secure the yarn and untwist the end of the yarn to create the hairy end of the tail.

Finishing
Sew the legs to the bottom part of the body, spacing them evenly around. Carefully pin the head to the neck and sew together using the Mattress Stitch. Sew the ears to the side of the head, and the two horns to the top of the head. Embroider nostrils with C2, and if not using safety eyes, embroider the eyes with C2. Sew the tail to the back of the body between the two back legs. Weave in ends.

Giraffe Chart 1

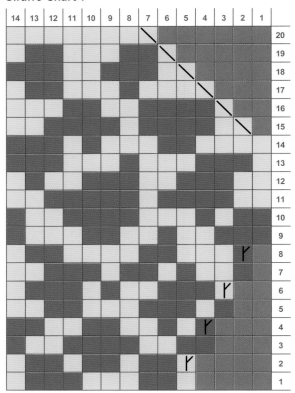

Giraffe Chart 2

Legend

No Stitch
Placeholder - No stitch made.

knit
knit stitch

kfb
Knit into the front and back of the stitch

ssk
Slip one stitch as if to knit, Slip another stitch as if to knit. Insert left-hand needle into front of these 2 stitches and knit them together

MC

C1

Giraffe Chart 3

10	9	8	7	6	5	4	3	2	1	
□	□	□	□	□	□	╲	■	□	□	24
□	□	■	■	□	□	□	□	■	□	23
□	□	■	■	□	□	□	□	■	□	22
□	□	□	■	■	□	□	□	■	□	21
■	■	□	■	□	□	□	■	■	□	20
■	■	□	■	□	□	□	□	■	□	19
□	■	□	□	□	□	□	□	■	□	18
□	□	□	■	■	□	□	□	■	□	17
□	□	■	■	■	□	╲	□	■	□	16
□	□	■	■	□	□	□	□	■	□	15
■	■	■	□	□	□	□	■	■	□	14
■	■	■	■	□	□	□	■	■	□	13
■	■	■	□	□	□	□	□	■	□	12
□	■	■	□	□	□	□	□	■	□	11
□	□	■	■	□	■	□	□	■	□	10
□	□	□	■	■	■	□	□	■	□	9
□	□	■	■	□	□	□	╲	■	□	8
■	■	□	■	□	□	□	□	■	□	7
■	■	■	□	□	□	□	□	■	□	6
□	□	■	□	□	□	□	□	■	□	5
□	□	□	■	■	■	□	□	□	□	4
□	□	■	■	□	■	■	□	□	□	3
□	■	■	□	□	□	□	□	□	□	2
□	■	■	□	□	□	□	□	□	□	1

Giraffe Chart 4

10	9	8	7	6	5	4	3	2	1	
□	□	■	■	□	□	□	■	□	□	10
□	■	■	□	■	□	□	■	■	□	9
□	■	■	□	□	□	□	□	■	□	8
□	■	■	□	□	□	□	■	■	□	7
□	□	□	□	□	■	■	■	□	□	6
■	■	■	□	□	□	□	■	■	□	5
■	■	■	□	□	□	■	■	□	□	4
□	□	■	□	□	□	■	■	□	□	3
□	□	□	□	■	■	□	■	■	□	2
□	□	□	□	□	□	□	□	□	□	1

HAPPY SHEEP HEADBAND

by Trelly Hernández

FINISHED MEASUREMENTS

Child (Adult): 17.5 (19)" circumference x 3.5" high

YARN

Knit Picks Wool of the Andes Superwash Worsted (100% Superwash Wool; 110 yards/50g): MC Fjord Heather 26316, C1 White 26326, C2 Coal 26323; 1 skein each

NEEDLES

US 2 (3mm) 16" circular needles, or 2 sizes smaller than needle to obtain gauge
US 4 (3.5mm) 16" circular needles, or size to obtain gauge

NOTIONS

Yarn Needle
Stitch Marker

GAUGE

22 sts and 32 rows = 4" in St st in the round with bigger needles, blocked

Happy Sheep Headband

Notes:

This headband is very easy to make with a simple chart to follow. Repeat each row of the chart 12 (13) times every round, reading them from right to left.

Ribbing Pattern (worked in the round over an even number of sts)

All Rnds: *K1 TBL, P1, repeat from * to end.

DIRECTIONS

With smaller needles and MC, CO 96 (104) sts, place marker and join in the round being careful not to twist your sts.

Work Ribbing Pattern for 8 rounds in total.

Change to bigger needles and work Chart 1 once.

Change to smaller needles and work Ribbing Pattern for 8 rounds in total.

Bind off the sts.

Finishing

Weave in ends, wash and block to finished measurements.

Happy Sheep Chart

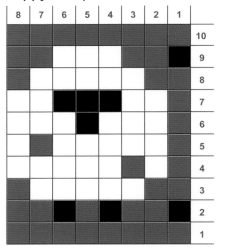

Legend

☐	**knit** knit stitch
■	MC
☐	C1
■	C2

HEART LACE MITTS

by Quenna Lee

FINISHED MEASUREMENTS

7.5-8.5 (8.5-9.25)" palm circumference; 7.75 (8.25)" long from bottom of cuff to top.

YARN

Knit Picks Hawthorne Fingering (80% Superwash Fine Highland Wool, 20% Polyamide (Nylon); 357 yards/100g): Rose City 26432, 1 hank

NEEDLES

US 4 (3.5mm) DPNs or two 24" circular needles for two circulars technique, or one 32" or longer circular needle for Magic Loop technique, or size to obtain gauge

NOTIONS

Yarn Needle
Stitch Markers
Scrap Yarn
#C crochet hook (optional; for finishing nupps)

GAUGE

20 sts and 36 rnds = 4" in K3 x P1 ribbing, blocked and stretched
3" across x 2" high = One rep of Lace pattern, blocked

Heart Lace Mitts

Notes:

Mitts are worked in the round from the bottom up, working the Lace Pattern twice. When the cuff is completed, the thumb gusset is formed with increases. The thumb stitches are placed on scrap yarn until the palm is completed, then the thumb sts are worked in the round.

When creating the nupps, use a very loose tension. They are finished on the following round by knitting the sts together through the back loops. A crochet hook can be used to finish them.

Lace pattern can be worked from the chart or text, read each chart row from right to left.

Lace Pattern (in the rnd over a multiple of 15 sts)
Rnd 1: P1, K4, K2tog, YO, P1, YO, SSK, K4, P1.
Rnd 2: (P1, K6) x 2, P1.
Rnd 3: P1, K3, K2tog, YO, K1, P1, K1, YO, SSK, K3, P1.
Rnd 4: P1, K4, (P1, K1) x 2, P1, K4, P1.
Rnd 5: P1, K2, K2tog, YO, (P1, K1) x 2, P1, YO, SSK, K2, P1.
Rnd 6: P1, K3, P2, K1, P1, K1, P2, K3, P1.
Rnd 7: P1, K1, K2tog, YO, P1, nupp, K1, P1, K1, nupp, P1, YO, SSK, K1, P1.
Rnd 8: P1, K2, P2, K5tog TBL, K1, P1, K1, K5tog TBL, P2, K2, P1.
Rnd 9: P1, K2tog, YO, P1, nupp, K2, P1, K2, nupp, P1, YO, SSK, P1.
Rnd 10: P1, K1, P2, K5tog TBL, K2, P1, K2, K5tog TBL, P2, K1, P1.
Rnd 11: P1, K1, P1, nupp, K3, P1, K3, nupp, P1, K1, P1.
Rnd 12: P1, K1, P1, K5tog TBL, K3, P1, K3, K5tog TBL, P1, K1, P1.
Rnd 13: P1, K1, nupp, K2, (P1, K1) x 2, P1, K2, nupp, K1, P1.
Rnd 14: P1, K1, K5tog TBL, K2, (P1, K1) x 2, P1, K2, K5tog TBL, K1, P1.
Rnd 15: Rep Rnd 1.
Rnd 16: Rep Rnd 3.
Rnd 17: P1, K2, K2tog, YO, K2, P1, K2, YO, SSK, K2, P1.
Rnd 18: P1, K1, K2tog, YO, K3, P1, K3, YO, SSK, K1, P1.
Rnd 19: P1, K2tog, YO, K4, P1, K4, YO, SSK, P1.
Rnd 20: Rep Rnd 2.

Nupp: Loosely (K1, YO) x 2, K1 in a single st (4 sts inc)
K5tog TBL: K5 sts together through the back loop

DIRECTIONS

CO 42 (46) sts. PM, join for working in the rnd being careful not to twist sts.

Cuff
Set-up Rnd: P1, K3 (5), P1, (K2, P2, K2, P1) twice, K3 (5), P1, * K3, P1, rep from * to last 3 sts, K3.
Work as established until cuff measures 2.75" from CO.

Thumb Gusset:
For Left Mitt only:
Set-up Rnd: M1R, K1, M1L, PM for thumb gusset, work pattern to end—2 gusset sts inc. 44 (48) sts.
Next Rnd: P1, K1, P1, SM, work in pattern to end.

Inc Rnd: P1, M1R, K to 1 st before M, M1L, P1, SM, K3 (5), work Lace pattern over 15 sts, K3 (5), work in pattern to end—2 gusset sts inc. 46 (50) sts.
Rnds 2-3: P1, K to 1 st before M, P1, SM, work in pattern to end.

For Right Mitt only:
Set-up Rnd: Work pattern for 22 (26) sts, PM, M1R, K1, M1L, PM for thumb gusset, work pattern to end—2 gusset sts inc. 44 (48) sts.
Next Rnd: Work in pattern to M, SM, P1, K1, P1, SM, work in pattern to end.

Inc Rnd: P1, K3 (5), work Lace pattern over 15 sts, K3 (5), SM, P1, M1R, K to 1 st before M, M1L, P1, SM, work in pattern to end—2 gusset sts inc. 46 (50) sts.
Rnds 2-3: Work to M, SM, P1, K to 1 st before M, P1, SM, work in pattern to end.

For both mitts:
Rep last 3 rnds 5 (6) more times. Rep Inc Rnd once. 58 (64) sts: 17 (19) sts between M for thumb gusset.

Work even, with no increases, until piece measures 3 (3.25)" from the base of the thumb gusset.

For Left Mitt only:
Next Rnd: Transfer 17 (19) thumb gusset sts to scrap yarn, removing thumb M. PM for beginning of rnd, with working yarn, CO 1 st, work in pattern to end. 42 (46) sts.

For Right Mitt only:
Next Rnd: Work to thumb M, remove M, transfer 17 (19) thumb gusset sts to scrap yarn, remove M, CO 1 st, work in pattern to end. 42 (46) sts.

For both mitts:
Work as established until Rnds 1-20 of Lace Pattern has been worked 2 times total.

Rib Edging
Edging Rnd: P1, K3 (5), P1, (K2, P2, K2, P1) twice, K3 (5), P1, * K3, P1, rep from * to last 3 sts, K3.
Rep Edging Rnd 3 (7) additional times.

BO off loosely in pattern.

Thumb
Transfer the held 17 (19) thumb sts to needle(s). Join yarn and PU and K 1 st from the CO st. PM, join for working in the rnd. 18 (20) sts.

Work in St st (K all rnds) for 6 (8) rnds.

Next 2 Rnds: *K1, P1, rep from * to end.

BO off loosely in pattern.

Finishing
Weave in ends, wash and block to size.

Lace Chart

15	14	13	12	11	10	9	8	7	6	5	4	3	2	1	
●							●							●	20
●	/	O					●					O	/	●	19
●		/	O				●				O	/		●	18
●			/	O			●			O	/			●	17
●				/	O		●		O	/				●	16
●					/	O	●	O	/					●	15
●		△5			●		●		●			△5		●	14
●		00			●		●		●			00		●	13
●		●	△5				●				△5	●		●	12
●		●	00				●				00	●		●	11
●		●	●	△5			●			△5	●	●		●	10
●	\	O	●	00			●			00	●	O	/	●	9
●			●	●	△5		●		△5	●	●			●	8
●	\		O	●	00		●		00	●	O	/		●	7
●				●	●		●		●	●				●	6
●			\	O	●		●		●	O	/			●	5
●					●		●		●					●	4
●				\	O	●	●		O	/				●	3
●							●							●	2
●				\	O	●	O	/						●	1

Legend

- **purl** — purl stitch (●)
- **knit** — knit stitch (☐)
- **k2tog** (/) — Knit two stitches together as one stitch
- **yo** (O) — yarn over
- **ssk** (\) — Slip one stitch as if to knit, slip another stitch as if to knit. Insert left-hand needle into front of these 2 stitches and knit them together
- **nupp** (00) — (k1 p1 k1 p1 k1) in stitch. 4 sts increased
- **k5tog** (△5) — Knit five stitches together through the back loop as one

HOUNDSTOOTH COWL

by Kay Meadors

FINISHED MEASUREMENTS
27" circumference x 8.5" high

YARN
Knit Picks Swish Worsted (100%
Superwash Merino Wool; 110 yards/50g):
MC: Black 23876, CC: Hollyberry 25148;
2 balls each

NEEDLES
US 5 (3.75 mm) 24" circular needle, or 3
sizes smaller than needle used to obtain
gauge.
US 8 (5.00 mm) 24" circular needle, or
size to obtain gauge

NOTIONS
Yarn Needle
Stitch Marker

GAUGE
19 sts and 20 rnds = 4" in Houndstooth
Pattern in the round on larger needles,
blocked

Houndstooth Cowl

Notes:

This cowl features the classic houndstooth stitch. It is worked in the round (knitting all sts) except for a garter turning ridge of CC on each end. This turning ridge gives a peek of color on the edge that finishes this design perfectly. The Cowl is folded to the WS on this turning ridge and hemmed in place.

When changing colors, do not carry yarn across more than 3 stitches; at the end of Rnd 2 of Houndstooth Chart or line-by-line instructions, overlap the MC after the last 3 sts before beginning the first 3 sts of Rnd 3 of Houndstooth Chart.
Read each chart rnd from right to left.
Maintain an even tension when changing colors.

Houndstooth Pattern (in the round over a multiple of 4 sts)
Round 1: * With MC K1, with CC K1, with MC K2; rep from * around.
Round 2: * With MC K1, with CC K3; rep from * around.
Round 3: * With CC K3, with MC K1; rep from * around.
Round 4: * With MC K2, with CC K1, with MC K1; rep from * around.
Rep Rnds 1-4 for pattern.

DIRECTIONS
Hem
With CC and smaller size circular needle, loosely CO 128 sts. Leave a long yarn tail, at least two times the length of CO, for sewing.

PM and begin working in the rnd, being careful not to twist sts.
Rnds 1-4: K in CC.

After last rnd, do not cut CC, instead catch CC loosely at back of work, every other round, until it is needed again.

Turning Ridge: With MC P.

Body
Knit 4 rnds in MC.
Change to larger size circular needle.
Work from Houndstooth Chart or written Houndstooth Pattern instruction, repeating Rnds 1-4 a total of nine times.

Work across Chart 32 times, knitting all sts.
Repeat Chart Rnds 1-4 a total of 9 times.

Change to smaller needle.

Do not cut CC, instead catch CC loosely at back of work, every other round, until it is needed again.
Knit 4 rnds in MC.
Cut MC.

Hem
Turning Ridge: With CC P.
Rnds 1-4: K.
BO off all sts loosely. Cut yarn, leaving a long tail, at least 2 times the circumference, for sewing.

Finishing
Fold Hem at purled turning ridge to WS of Cowl. Using long yarn tail, whipstitch hem in place, catching every other stitch.

Repeat for Hem on other end. Weave in ends, wash and block to finished measurements.

Houndstooth Chart

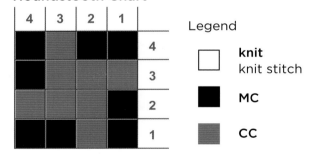

Legend
knit **knit stitch**
MC
CC

KEARSARGE SHAWL

by Kathi Snodgrass

FINISHED MEASUREMENTS

28" back depth, 60" wide at widest point, after blocking

YARN

Knit Picks Diadem Solid DK (50% Baby Alpaca, 50% Mulberry Silk; 219 yards/100g): Copper Solid 26352, 2 hanks

NEEDLES

US 10 (6 mm) 32" circular needles, or size to obtain gauge

NOTIONS

Yarn needle

GAUGE

18 sts and 24 rows = 4" in St st, blocked lightly. (Gauge for this project is approximate)

Kearsarge Shawl

Notes:

The Kearsarge Shawl is named for a pass in the eastern Sierra mountain range. Once you hike to the summit, the peaks of the Sierras open up as far as you can see. It is a passage into several national parks including Kings Canyon, and the John Muir Trail.

The shawl begins with a few stitches and grows with each right side row into a triangular shawl. Because of the construction, the shawl can be as small or large as the knitter would like. Knit out of a DK weight and larger than normal needles shawl grows quickly. The pattern is charted as well as written out. Follow RS chart rows from right to left, and WS chart rows from left to right. The lace patterning is only on the right side, with the wrong side knit with a garter edge and purled stitches. It is perfect to knit out of a special luxury yarn with nice drape.

Skp2: Sl 1, K2tog, pass slipped st over K2tog. 2 sts dec.

DIRECTIONS

CO 3 sts. Work Rows 1-21 of Chart A (knit flat), or follow written directions, below.

Row 1 (WS): Knit. (3 sts)
Row 2 (RS): (K1, YO) x 2, K1. (5 sts)
Row 3: Knit.
Row 4: K2, YO, K1, YO, K2. (7 sts)
Row 5: K3, P1, K3.
Row 6: K2, YO, K3, YO, K2. (9 sts)
Rows 7, 9, 11, 13, 15, 17, 19: K3, P to the last 3 sts, K3.
Row 8: K2, YO, K1, M1R, K3, M1L, K1, YO, K2. (13 sts)
Row 10: K2, YO, K2, K2tog, YO, K1, YO, SSK, K2, YO, K2. (15 sts)
Row 12: K2, YO, K1, M1R, K1, K2tog, YO, K3, YO, SSK, K1, M1L, K1, YO, K2. (19 sts)
Row 14: K2, YO, K3, K2tog, YO, K5, YO, SSK, K3, YO, K2. (21 sts)
Row 16: K2, YO, K3, K2tog, YO, K7, YO, SSK, K3, YO, K2. (23 sts)
Row 18: K2, YO, K1 (K2, K2tog, YO) x2, K1, (YO, SSK, K2) x2, K1, YO, K2. (25 sts)
Row 20: K2, YO, K1, (K2, K2tog, YO) x2, K3, (YO, SSK, K2) x2, K1, YO, K2. (27 sts)
Row 21: K3, P to the last 3 sts, K3.

Work Rows 1-24 of Chart B six times or until desired depth, or follow written directions, below.

Row 1 (RS): K2, YO, K1, M1R, K1, K2tog, YO, K1, *YO, SSK, K9, K2tog, YO, K1, rep from * until 6 sts remain, YO, SSK, K1, M1L, K1, YO, K2. 4 sts inc.
Row 2 and all WS rows through Row 24: K3, P to the last 3 sts, K3.
Row 3: K2, YO, K3, K2tog, YO, K2, *K1, YO, SSK, K7, K2tog, YO, K2, rep from * until 8 sts remain, K1, YO, SSK, K3, YO, K2. 2 sts inc.
Row 5: K2, YO, K3, K2tog, YO, K3, *K2, YO, SSK, K5, K2tog, YO, K3 rep from * until 9 sts remain, K2, YO, SSK, K3, YO, K2. 2 sts inc.
Row 7: K2, YO, K3, K2tog, YO, K4, *K3, YO, SSK, K3, K2tog, YO, K4, rep from * until 10 sts remain, K3, YO, SSK, K3, YO, K2. 2 sts

inc.
Row 9: K2, YO, K3, K2tog, YO, K2, K2tog, YO, K1, *YO, SSK, K2, YO, SSK, K1, K2tog, YO, K2, K2tog, YO, K1, rep from * until 11 sts remain, (YO, SSK, K2) x2, K1, YO, K2. 2 sts inc.
Row 11: K2, YO, K3, (K2tog, YO, K2) x 2, *K1, YO, SSK, K2, YO, Skp2, YO, K2, K2tog, YO, K2, rep from * until 12 sts remain, (K1, YO, SSK, K1) x2, K2, YO, K2. 2 sts inc.
Row 13: K2, YO, K1, M1R, K1, K2tog, YO, K1, YO, SSK, K5, *K4, K2tog, YO, K1, YO, SSK, K5, rep from * until 13 sts remain, K4, K2tog, YO, K1, YO, SSK, K1, M1L, K1, YO, K2. 4 sts inc.
Row 15: K2, YO, K3, K2tog, YO, K3, YO, SSK, K4, *K3, K2tog, YO, K3, YO, SSK, K4, rep from * until 15 sts remain, K3, K2tog, YO, K3, YO, SSK, K3, YO, K2. 2 sts inc.
Row 17: K2, YO, K1, *K2, K2tog, YO, K5, YO, SSK, K3, rep from * until 2 sts remain, YO, K2. 2 sts inc.
Row 19: K2, YO, K2, *K1, K2tog, YO, K7, YO, SSK, K2, rep from * until 3 sts remain, K1, YO, K2. 2 sts inc.
Row 21: K2, YO, K3, *K2tog, YO, K2, K2tog, YO, K1, YO, SSK, K2, YO, SSK, K1, rep from * until 4 sts remain, K2, YO, K2. 2 sts inc.
Row 23: K2, YO, K3, K2tog, *YO, K2, K2tog, YO, K3, YO, SSK, K2, YO, Skp2, rep from * until 18 sts remain, YO, K2, K2tog, YO, K3, YO, SSK, K2, YO, SSK, K3, YO, K2. 2 sts inc.

Repeat Rows 1-24 five more times, or until desired depth.

Knit 4 rows.

BO loosely.

Finishing

Weave in ends but do not snip until after blocking, wash and block to size.

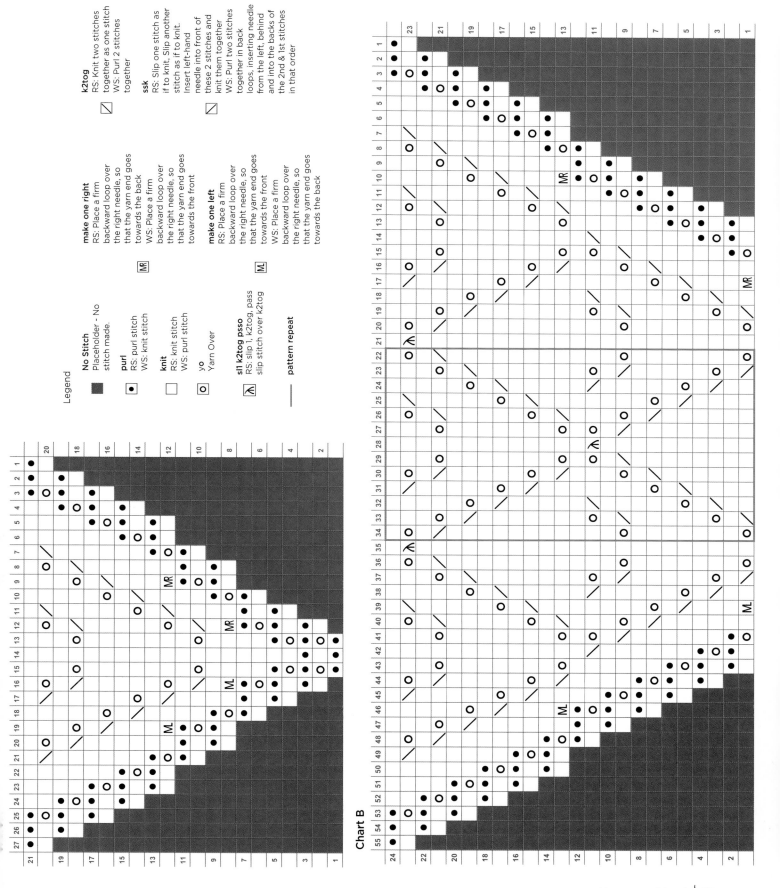

Legend

No Stitch
Placeholder - No stitch made.

purl
RS: purl stitch
WS: knit stitch

knit
RS: knit stitch
WS: purl stitch

yo
Yarn Over

sl1 k2tog psso
RS: slip 1, k2tog, pass slip stitch over k2tog

— **pattern repeat**

k2tog
RS: Knit two stitches together as one stitch
WS: Purl 2 stitches together

ssk
RS: Slip one stitch as if to knit, Slip another stitch as if to knit. Insert left-hand needle into front of these 2 stitches and knit them together
WS: Purl two stitches together in back loops, inserting needle from the left, behind and into the backs of the 2nd & 1st stitches in that order

make one right
RS: Place a firm backward loop over the right needle, so that the yarn end goes towards the back
WS: Place a firm backward loop over the right needle, so that the yarn end goes towards the front

M̄R

make one left
RS: Place a firm backward loop over the right needle, so that the yarn end goes towards the front
WS: Place a firm backward loop over the right needle, so that the yarn end goes towards the back

M̄L

Chart B

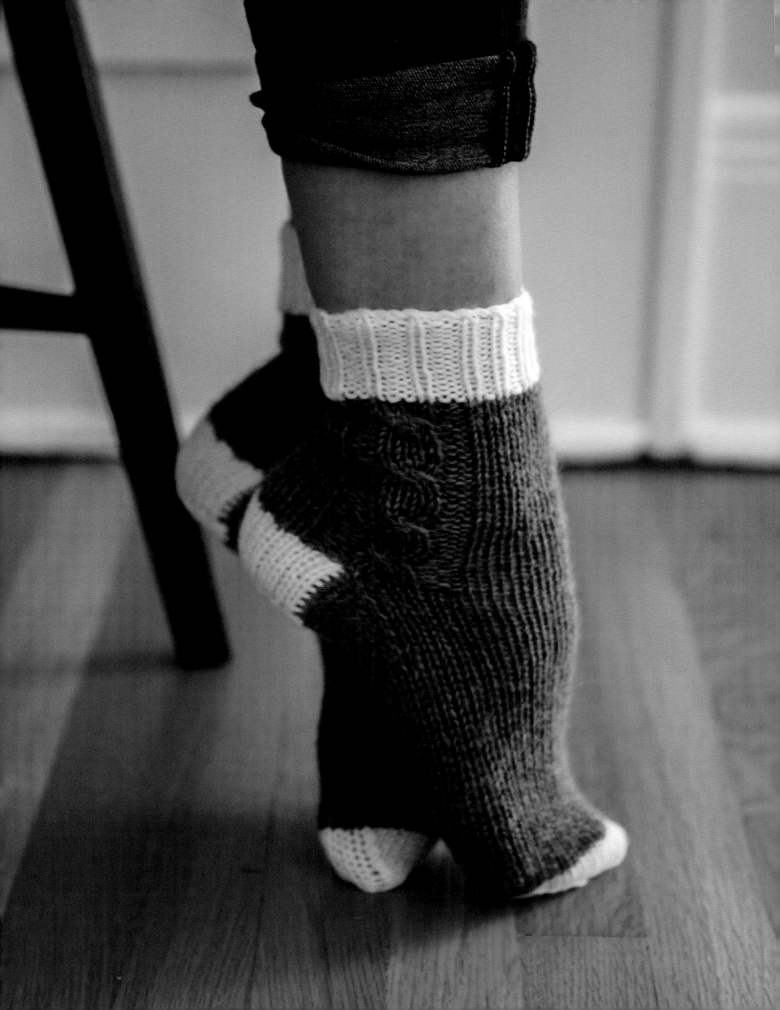

LAZY WEEKEND SOCKS

by Brenda Castiel

FINISHED MEASUREMENTS

S (M, L): 6″ leg length x 6.5 (7.25, 8)″ foot circumference x 8.75 (9.5, 10.5)″ foot length

YARN

Knit Picks Wool of the Andes Superwash Worsted (100% Superwash Wool; 110 yards/50g): MC Pampas Heather 26314, 2 balls; C1 White 26326, 1 ball

NEEDLES

US 4 (3.5mm) DPNs, or 2 circular needles for Two Circular Method, or 2 sizes smaller than needle to obtain gauge, US 6 (4mm) DPNs, or 2 circular needles for Two Circular Method, or size to obtain gauge

NOTIONS

Cable Needle
Yarn Needle
Stitch Markers

GAUGE

22 sts and 30 rows = 4″ in St st in the round on larger needles, blocked

Lazy Weekend Socks

Notes:

These chunky socks are perfect for lounging around the house on a lazy weekend while reading and sipping a hot beverage.

C4F – Cable 4 Front
Sl 2 sts to the CN and hold in front of work. K next 2 sts, and then K the 2 sts from the CN. This will result in a cable that crosses to the left.

C4B – Cable 4 Back
Sl 2 sts to the CN and hold in back of work. K next 2 sts, and then K the 2 sts from the CN. This will result in a cable that crosses to the right.

DIRECTIONS
First Sock
Leg

Using smaller needles, and C1, CO 37 (41, 45) sts very loosely. Divide sts over 4 smaller DPNs as follows: 9 (10, 11) sts on each of 3 needles, and 10 (11, 12) on the last. For working on 2 circular needles, place 18 (20, 22) sts on needle 1 and 19 (21, 23) on needle 2.

Join to work in round, being careful not to twist. PM to mark beginning of rnd.

Leg rib pattern: (P2, K1) twice, P2, *K1, P1. Rep from * to last st, K1. Work leg in rib pattern in C1, until it measures 2" from CO edge.

Change to MC and larger needles.

Round 1: K to last 2 sts, K2tog. 36 (40, 44) sts.
Round 2: P2, K4, P2, K to end.
Rounds 3-5: Rep Round 2.
Round 6: P2, C4F, P2, K to end.
Rounds 7-9: Rep Round 2.

Repeat Rounds 2-9 until leg measures about 6" from CO edge, ending with Round 9.

Heel Flap

Move beginning of rnd marker 4 sts to the left (to the center of the cable).

Rearrange sts on needles as follows: For DPNs, Needle 1 has first 9 (10, 11) sts after new beginning of rnd marker, Needle 2 has next 9 (10, 11) sts, and Needle 3 has remaining 18 (20, 22) sts. Knit sts around, stopping at beginning of Needle 3, ready to work heel flap. For 2 circular needles, Needle 1 has first 18 (20, 22) sts after new beginning of rnd marker, Needle 2 has remaining sts. Knit sts around, stopping at beginning of Needle 2, ready to work heel flap.

Change to C1.
With RS facing, work back and forth on heel sts as follows:
Row 1 (RS): *Sl 1 P-wise, K1, rep from * to end.
Row 2 (WS): Sl 1 P-wise, P to end.

Repeat Rows 1-2 until 18 (22, 24) rows are complete, or heel flap measures 2 (2.25, 2.5)", ending with a WS row.

Turn Heel

Row 1 (RS): K10 (11, 12) Ssk, K1. Turn.
Row 2 (WS): Sl 1, P3 (3, 3) P2tog, P1. Turn.
Row 3: Sl 1, K4 (4, 4) Ssk, K1. Turn.
Row 4: Sl 1, P5 (5, 5) P2tog, P1. Turn.
Row 5: Sl 1, K6 (6, 6) Ssk, K1. Turn.
Row 6: Sl 1, P7 (7, 7) P2tog, P1. Turn.
Follow the directions that correspond to your size:

Small size only:
Row 7: Sl 1, K8, Ssk. Turn.
Row 8: Sl 1, P8, P2tog. Turn.
10 sts remain.

Medium size only:
Row 7: Sl 1, K8, Ssk, K1. Turn.
Row 8: Sl 1, P9, P2tog, P1. Turn.
12 sts remain.

Large size only:
Row 7: Sl 1, K8, Ssk, K1. Turn.
Row 8: Sl 1, P9, P2tog, P1. Turn.
Row 9: Sl 1, K10, Ssk. Turn.
Row 10: Sl 1, P10, P2tog. Turn.
12 sts remain.

All sizes:
Work 5 (6, 6) sts. PM for new beginning of rnd.
Change back to MC.

Heel Gusset

In following sections, if using 2 circular needles, Needle 1 equates to Needle 1 and Needle 2 DPNs; Needle 2 equates to Needle 3 and 4 DPNs.
Knit remaining 5 (6, 6) heel sts. [Needle 1]
Continuing with the same needle, PU and K 9 (11, 12) sts along the side of the heel.
On same needle, PU and K a st from row below the first instep st to prevent a hole. [Needle 1: 15 (18, 19) sts total]
With a free needle, K across 9 (10, 11) instep sts. [Needle 2]
With a free needle, K across 9 (10, 11) instep sts. [Needle 3]
With free needle, PU and K a st from row below the last instep st to prevent a hole.
With same needle, PU and K 9 (11, 12) sts along side of the heel and K across 5 (6, 6) remaining heel sts to end at beginning of rnd. [Needle 4: 15 (18, 19) sts total]

Shape Gusset
Round 1(Dec Round):
Needle 1: K to last 3 sts, K2tog, K1.
Needle 2: (Instep) Knit.
Needle 3: (Instep) Knit.
Needle 4: K1, Ssk, K to end.
Round 2: Knit.
Rep Rounds 1 and 2 until 36 (40, 44) sts remain.

Foot

Continue working even in rounds until foot measures 7.5 (8.25, 8.75)" from base of heel, or 1.25 (1.25, 1.5)" less than desired length of foot.

End at beginning of rnd.

Change to C1.

Shape Toe
Round 1 (Dec Round):
Needle 1: (Sole) K to last 3 sts, K2tog, K1.
Needle 2: (Instep) K1, Ssk, K to end.
Needle 3: (Instep) K to last 3 sts, K2tog, K1.
Needle 4: (Sole) K1, Ssk, K to end.
Round 2: Knit.
Repeat Rounds 1 and 2 until 24 (28, 28) total sts remain.
Work Decrease Round 1 only until 12 sts remain. 6 instep sts, 6 sole sts.

Finishing
Work sts on Needle 1. Sl sts from Needle 4 to opposite end of Needle 1.
Sl sts from Needle 3 onto Needle 2.
If using 2 circular needles, arrange sts so that 6 instep sts are on one needle, 6 sole sts are on second needle.
Holding two needles together, graft sts using Kitchener Stitch.
Weave in ends, block.

Second Sock
Leg
Work Leg as for first Sock, except use C4B instead of C4F.

Heel Flap
Move beginning of rnd marker 22 (24, 26) sts to the left (opposite to the cable).
Rearrange sts on needles as follows:
For DPNs, Needle 1 has first 9 (10, 11) sts after new beginning of rnd marker, Needle 2 has next 9 (10, 11) sts, and Needle 3 has remaining 18 (20, 22) sts. Knit sts around, stopping at beginning of Needle 3, ready to work heel flap.

For 2 circular needles, Needle 1 has first 18 (20, 22) sts after new beginning of rnd marker, Needle 2 has remaining sts. Knit sts around, stopping at beginning of Needle 2, ready to work heel flap.

Change to C1.
Work the rest of the sock same as the first.

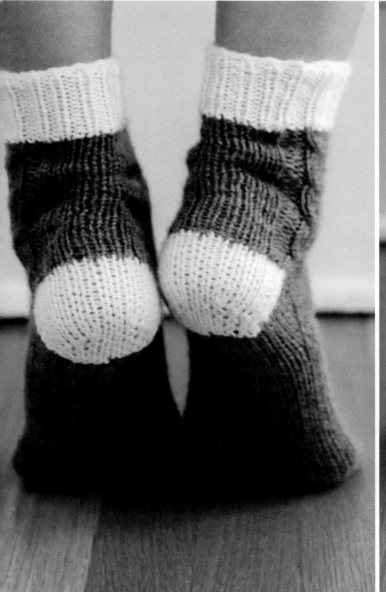

DAYA HEADBAND

by Allison O'Mahony

FINISHED MEASUREMENTS
18" circumference, 5" at widest point,
3.75" at narrowest point, after grafting

YARN
Knit Picks Super Tuff Puff (100% Wool; 44
yards/200g): Pomegranate 26848, 1 ball

NEEDLES
US 15 (10mm) straight or circular needles,
or size to obtain gauge
If using a circular needle, an additional
needle will be needed to hold the
provisional cast on stitches for grafting

NOTIONS
Cable needle
Yarn needle
Scrap yarn
T-pins
Blocking wires (optional but strongly
recommended)

GAUGE
9 sts and 17 rows = 4" over St st, blocked

Daya Headband

Notes:

This headband is knit flat from end to end. A provisional cast on allows the ends to be grafted together seamlessly. Follow the chart from right to left on RS rows (even numbers), and left to right on WS rows (odd numbers).

Provisional Cast On

A provisional cast on is a method that uses a length of waste yarn to hold live stitches so that they can be worked later. For help casting on provisionally, please refer to the following tutorial: http://tutorials.knitpicks.com/wptutorials/traditional-provisional/

3/3 Left Cross (3/3 LC)

Slip 3 sts onto CN, hold in front of work, K the next 3 sts, then K the sts on the CN.

Kitchener Stitch

For information on Kitchener Stitch, or "grafting", please refer to the following tutorial, paying close attention to follow the instructions specific to garter stitch: http://tutorials.knitpicks.com/wptutorials/kitchener-stitch/

Cable Pattern

Row 1 (RS): K4, 3/3 LC, K1. (11 sts)
Row 2 (WS): K4, P3, K4.
Row 3: Knit.
Rows 4 - 5: Repeat rows 2 - 3.
Row 6: Repeat row 2.
Row 7: Repeat row 1.
Row 8: K1, P3, K7.
Row 9: K1, 3/3 LC, K4.
Row 10: K1, P3, K3, P3, K1.
Row 11: Knit.
Row 12: Repeat row 10.
Row 13: Repeat row 1.
Row 14: K7, P3, K1.
Row 15: Repeat row 9.
Row 16: Repeat row 2.
Row 17: Knit.
Rows 18 - 19: Repeat rows 16 - 17.
Row 20: Repeat row 2.
Row 21: Repeat row 9.
Row 22: Knit.

DIRECTIONS

CO 11 sts using the Provisional Cast On.

Begin working in Garter stitch (K every row). Work until piece measures 5" from the CO edge.

Work Rows 1-22 of Cable Pattern (chart or written instructions).

Resume working in Garter stitch. Work until piece measures 17" from the CO edge, ending on a RS row.

Last Row (WS): K4, K2tog, K to end. (10 sts)

Finishing

Place the live sts onto waste yarn. Block the piece flat to finished measurements.

Unzip the Provisional CO (due to the nature of the Provisional CO, there will be 10 live sts). Place the live sts at both ends of the piece onto separate needles, remove the waste yarn, and use Kitchener Stitch to graft the sts together.

Weave in ends.

Cable Chart

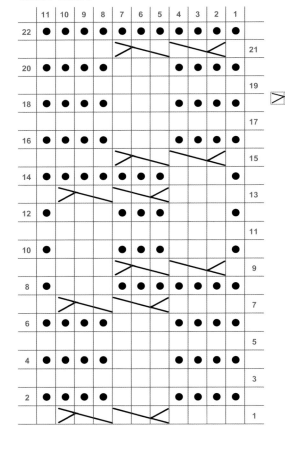

Legend

knit
RS: knit stitch
WS: purl stitch

3/3 LC
sl3 to CN, hold in front. k3, k3 from CN

purl
RS: purl stitch
WS: knit stitch

LEANAN HAT

by Stephannie Tallent

FINISHED MEASUREMENTS

17.25 (20.5, 24)" circumference (unstretched) x 8.25 (8.75, 9)" tall

YARN

Knit Picks City Tweed Aran/HW (55% Merino Wool, 25% Superfine Alpaca, 20% Donegal tweed; 164 yards/100g): Blue Blood 24529, 1 (1, 2) balls

NEEDLES

US 7 (4.5mm) DPNs or two 24" circular needles for two circulars technique, or one 32" or longer circular needle for Magic Loop technique, or size to obtain gauge
US 6 (4mm) DPNs or two 24" circular needles for two circulars technique, or one 32" or longer circular needle for Magic Loop technique, or one size smaller than needles used to obtain gauge

NOTIONS

Yarn Needle
Stitch Markers
Cable Needle
Pom Pom Maker (optional)

GAUGE

21 sts and 26 rows = 4" in Cable Pattern in the round on larger needles, unstretched, blocked.

Leanan Hat

Notes:

This hat is worked in the round from the K2, P2 ribbed brim up. Top it with an optional pom pom. Use a tubular cast on if desired.

Read chart from right to left.

K2, P2 Rib

All Rnds: *K2, P2; rep from * to end of rnd.

Lki: Lift the st 2 rows below the last st onto the left needle and knit this stitch. 1 st inc.

Rki: Lift the st 1 row below the next st onto the left needle and knit this stitch. 1 st inc.

Regular Cables

1/1 LCp: Sl 1 st to CN and hold in front; P1; K1 from CN.

1/1 RC: Sl 1 st to CN and hold in back; K1; K1 from CN.

1/1 RCp: Sl 1 st to CN and hold in back; K1; P1 from CN.

2/1 LC: Sl 2 sts to CN and hold in front; K1; K2 from CN.

2/1 LCp: Sl 2 sts to CN and hold in front; P1; K2 from CN.

2/1 RC: Sl 1 st to CN and hold in back; K2; K1 from CN.

2/1 RCp: Sl 1 st to CN and hold in back; K2; P1 from CN.

2/2 LC: Sl 2 sts to CN and hold in front; K2; K2 from CN.

2/2 LCp: Sl 2 sts to CN and hold in front; P2; K2 from CN.

2/2 RC: Sl 2 sts to CN and hold in back; K2; K2 from CN.

2/2 RCp: Sl 2 sts to CN and hold in back; K2; P2 from CN.

Decrease Cables

2/1 RCP2tog: Sl 1 st to CN, hold in back. K2. Sl purl st from CN back to LH needle. P2tog.

1/1 LPC decr: Sl st to RH needle. Sl 1 st to CN, hold in back. Sl st from RH needle to LH needle, P2tog. Sl st from CN to LH needle, P2tog. 2 sts dec.

2/1 LCP2tog: Sl purl st prior to cross to RH needle. Sl 2 sts to CN, hold in front; Sl purl st back to LH needle. P2tog. K2 from CN.

DIRECTIONS

Brim

CO 80 (96, 112) sts with smaller needles. Join in the round, being careful not to twist; PM for beginning of round.

Work K2, P2 Rib for 1 (3, 5) rnds.

Main Body

Rnds 1-4: Work Leanan Hat Chart 5 (6, 7) times around. 90 (108, 126) sts after Rnd 2.

Rnd 5: Change to larger needles. Continue working Leanan Hat chart 5 (6, 7) times around.

Complete Leanan Hat Chart.

Cut yarn, leaving a 6" tail. Thread yarn through live sts and pull snugly to close hole at top of hat.

Finishing

Weave in ends, wash and block.

Attach pom pom to top of hat if desired. See tutorial for making pom poms here: http://tutorials.knitpicks.com/wptutorials/how-to-make-pom-poms-with-the-clover-pom-pom-maker/.

Leanan Hat Chart

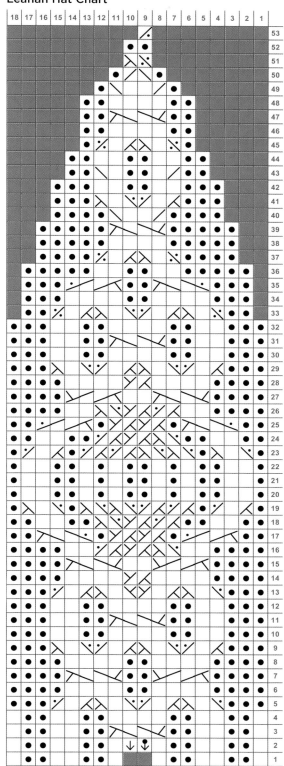

Legend

□	**knit** knit stitch
•	**purl** purl stitch
■	**No Stitch** Placeholder - No stitch made.
⬇	**LKI** Lift the st 2 rows below the last st onto the left needle and knit this stitch. 1 st inc.
↓	**RKI** Lift the st 1 row below the next st onto the left needle and knit this stitch. 1 st inc
(2/2 LC symbol)	**2/2 LC** sl 2 to CN, hold in front. k2, k2 from CN
(2/1 LCp symbol)	**2/1 LCp** sl2 to CN, hold in front. p1, k2 from CN
(2/1 RCp symbol)	**2/1 RCp** sl1 to CN, hold in back. k2, p1 from CN
(2/2 RC symbol)	**2/2 RC** sl2 to CN, hold in back. k2, k2 from CN
(2/1 RC symbol)	**2/1 RC** sl1 to CN, hold in back. k2, k1 from CN
(2/1 LC symbol)	**2/1 LC** sl2 to CN, hold in front. k1, k2 from CN
(1/1 RC symbol)	**1/1 RC** Sl 1 st to CN and hold in back. K1, K1 from CN
(1/1 LCp symbol)	**1/1 LCp** sl1 to CN, hold in front. p1. k1 from CN
(1/1 RCp symbol)	**1/1 RCp** sl1 to CN, hold in back. k1, p1 from CN
(2/2 RCp symbol)	**2/2 RCp** sl2 to CN, hold in back. k2, p2 from CN
(2/2 LCp symbol)	**2/2 LCp** sl 2 to CN, hold in front. p2, k2 from CN
(k2tog symbol)	**k2tog** Knit two stitches together as one stitch
(ssk symbol)	**ssk** Slip one stitch as if to knit, slip another stitch as if to knit. Insert left-hand needle into front of these 2 stitches and knit them together
(p2tog symbol)	**p2tog** Purl 2 stitches together
(2/1 LCp2tog symbol)	**2/1 LCp2tog** Sl purl st prior to cross to RH needle. Sl 2 sts to CN, hold in front; Sl purl st back to LH needle. P2tog. K2 from CN
(2/1 RCp2tog symbol)	**2/1 RCp2tog** Sl 1 st to CN, hold in back. K2. Sl purl st from CN back to LH needle. P2tog
(1/1 LPC decr symbol)	**1/1 LPC decr** Sl st to RH needle. Sl 1 st to CN, hold in back. Sl st from RH needle to LH needle, P2tog. Sl st from CN to LH needle, P2tog. 2 sts dec

LOTTIE'S BOOTIES

by Lisa Seifert

FINISHED MEASUREMENTS

3.75 (4, 4.5)" from heel to toe; bootie is meant to be worn with up to .5" of negative ease, to fit 0-3 months, (3-6 months, 6-12 months)

YARN

Knit Picks Swish Worsted (100% Superwash Merino Wool; 110 yards/50g): Dove Heather 25631, 1 ball

NEEDLES

US 4 (3.5mm) DPNs, or size to obtain gauge
US 2 (2.75mm) DPNs, or 2 sizes smaller than needles to obtain gauge

NOTIONS

Yarn Needle
Stitch Marker

GAUGE

24 sts and 30 rows = 4" in St st on larger needles, unblocked

Lottie's Booties

Notes:

These adorable wee booties are knit seamlessly from the cuff down. After knitting the ribbed cuff rows flat, booties are joined to knit the ankle in the round before the upper is worked flat in box stitch rows to desired length. Stitches are picked up along the sides and joined with the live heel stitches; bootie is then knit in stockinette, again in the round. The sole is knit and decreased in garter stitch until, finally, the remaining sole stitches are joined using Kitchener stitch. If desired, instructions are included for an I-cord tie that can be woven through (optional) yarn-over eyelets at the ankle to help keep booties in place. Cuff, ankle, and I-cord ties are knit using smaller needles; upper, sides, and soles are knit using larger needles.

Kitchener Stitch Bind-off

Set up: Arrange remaining sole sts lengthwise (remove M) so that there is an even number on two DPNs. Working from right to left, whether yarn is coming from the back or front needle, pass the yarn needle P-wise through the first st on the front DPN and then K-wise through the first st on the back DPN. Work remaining sts as follows:

Step 1: Insert the yarn needle K-wise through the first st on the front DPN and slide this st off DPN.
Step 2: Insert the yarn needle P-wise through the next st on the front DPN leaving st on DPN.
Step 3: Insert the yarn needle K-wise through the first st on the back DPN and slide this st off DPN.
Step 4: Insert the yarn needle P-wise through the next st on the back DPN leaving st on DPN.
Continue working Steps 1-4 until 1 st remains on each DPN; work steps 1 & 3; use tip of yarn needle to adjust/tighten sts as needed. Push yarn needle through sole to inside of bootie; cut yarn and weave in end.

I-Cord Ankle Tie (Make 2)

Using smaller needles, CO 3 sts, K3; *slide sts from left end of DPN to right end without turning work, K3*; repeat between ** until work is 16 (17, 18)" in length; BO. Cut yarn. Thread end of yarn onto yarn needle and weave through ankle eyelets; weave in ends.

Yarn-over Eyelets

Work on ankle rounds 15 (17, 19):

0-3 months: SM, K1, P2, YO, K2tog, P2, YO, K2tog, P2, YO, K2tog, P2, K2tog, YO, P2, K2tog, YO, P2, K2tog, YO, P2, K1.

3-6 (6-12) months: SM, K1, P2, YO, K2tog, P2, YO, K2tog, P2, YO, K2tog, P2, YO, K2tog, YO, P2, K2tog, YO, P2, K2tog, YO, P2, K2tog, P2, K1.

DIRECTIONS

Using smaller needles, CO 28 (32, 32) sts using long tail method.

Cuff

Row 1 (RS): K3, *P2, K2*; repeat between ** until 5 sts remain, P2, K3.
Row 2 (WS): P3, *K2, P2*; repeat between ** until 5 sts remain, K2, P3.
Rows 3-8 (10, 12): Repeat Rows 1 & 2 three (4, 5) times.

Ankle

Set up for ankle by dividing Cuff sts over 4 needles as follows:
Needle 1: Sl 5 sts P-wise.
Needle 2: Sl 10 (12, 12) sts P-wise.
Needle 3: Sl 8 (10, 10) sts P-wise.
Needle 4: 5 sts remain on needle 4. (Space between needles 1 & 4 becomes front center of bootie; PM and join to knit in the round on WS following instructions below. Rows are now called rounds.)

Work Rounds 9 (11, 13) – 20 (22, 24) as follows (if optional I-cord tie is desired, follow instructions for Yarn-over Eyelets):

Round 9 (11, 13): K 5 sts from needle 1 onto needle 4 as follows: K1, P2, K2 (needle 4 is now needle 1); work even around ankle to final st, K1.
Rounds 10 (12, 14) – 19 (21, 23): SM, K1, *P2, K2*; repeat between ** until 3 sts remain, P2, K1.
Round 20 (22, 24): SM, P1, K4, *P2, K2*; repeat between ** until 2 sts remain on needle 3, P2.

Upper

Row 1: With larger needles K4, P1, remove M, P1, K4, K first st from needle 2, turn (11 sts on needle).
Row 2: P5, K2, P4, P first st from needle 3, turn (12 sts on needle).
Row 3: K3, P2, K2, P2, K3, turn.
Row 4: P3, K2, P2, K2, P3, turn.
Row 5: K5, P2, K5, turn.
Row 6: P5, K2, P5, turn.

For size 0-3 months: Repeat rows 3-6 (10 rows total).
For size 3-6 months: Repeat rows 3-6, then repeat rows 3-4 (12 rows total).
For size 6-12 months: Repeat rows 3-6 twice (14 rows total).

Shape Toe (sizes 0-3 & 6-12 months)
Row 11 (15): K2, SSK, P1, K2, P1, K2tog, K2 (2 sts dec).
Row 12 (16): P3, K1, P2, K1, P3.
Row 13 (17): K2, SSK, P2, K2tog, K2 (2 sts dec).
Row 14 (18): P3, K2, P3.
Row 15 (19): K2, SSK, K2tog, K2 (2 sts dec).

Shape Toe (size 3-6 months)
Row 13: K2, SSK, K1, P2, K1, K2tog, K2 (2 sts dec).
Row 14: P4, K2, P4.
Row 15: K2, SSK, K2, K2tog, K2 (2 sts dec).
Row 16: P all sts.
Row 17: K2, SSK, K2tog, K2 (2 sts dec).

Sides

Set-up:
Needle 1: DPN with 6 remaining toe sts becomes needle 1.
Needle 2: Evenly PU and K15 (14, 15) sts along left edge of upper, K5 (6, 6) reserved heel sts.
Needle 3: K3 (4, 4), PM, K3 (4, 4). M is placed now, but ignore it until working sole.
Needle 4: K5 (6, 6), PU and K15 (14, 15) sts along right edge of upper. 52 (54, 56) sts.

Work in St st for 5 (6, 7) rounds, ending with needle 4; cut yarn.

Sole

Round 1: Sl 3 (4, 4) heel sts P-wise, SM, join yarn, P to M.

Rounds 2-3: Remove M, Sl 1 P-wise WYIB, PM, P to M.

Round 4: SM, K to M.

Round 5: Heel: SM, *P until 1 st remains, Sl first st from next DPN P-wise onto current DPN, P2tog* (6 heel sts total). **Right Side:** repeat between **. **Toe:** Sl st just made onto new DPN, repeat between ** (6 toe sts total). **Left Side:** repeat between **. **Heel:** Sl st just made onto new DPN, P to M (4 sts dec).

Round 6: Heel: SM, *K until 1 st remains, Sl first st from next DPN P-wise onto current DPN, K2tog* (6 heel sts total). **Right Side:** repeat between **. **Toe:** Sl st just made onto new DPN, repeat between ** (6 toe sts total). **Left Side:** repeat between **. **Heel:** Sl st just made onto new DPN, K to M (4 sts dec).

Round 7: Repeat Round 5.

Round 8: Repeat Round 6.

Round 9: Repeat Round 5.

Round 10: Repeat Round 6.

Round 11: Repeat Round 5 until 3 sts remain on needle 1.

Finishing

Cut yarn leaving a 12" tail; thread yarn onto yarn needle, and BO remaining sts using Kitchener Stitch Bind-off. Weave in ends. If desired, gently sew cuff down to keep it in place. LIghtly block, if desired, before weaving in optional I-cord tie.

AUTUMN ARBOR HAT

by Faye Kennington

FINISHED MEASUREMENTS
19.25 (21.25, 23.5)" circumference at brim x 10.5 (11.25, 12)" deep

YARN
Knit Picks Palette (100% Peruvian Highland Wool; 231 yards/50g): MC Cream 23730, 1 (1, 2) balls; C1 Rainforest Heather 24008, 1 ball; C2 Salsa Heather 24003, 1 ball

NEEDLES
US 1 (2.5mm) 16" circular needles and DPNs, or two 24" circular needles for two circulars technique, or one 32" or longer circular needle for Magic Loop technique, or size to obtain gauge

US 2 (2.75mm) 16" circular needles, or two 24" circular needles for two circulars technique, or one 32" or longer circular needle for Magic Loop technique, or size to obtain gauge

NOTIONS
Yarn Needle
1 Stitch Marker
Pom-Pom Maker, Large

GAUGE
30 sts and 36 rows = 4" in St st in the round with smaller needles, blocked
30 sts and 32 rows = 4" in stranded St st in the round with larger needles, blocked

Autumn Arbor Hat

Notes:

This hat is knit in the round from the brim to crown. Larger needles are used for working the basic tree chart to guard against tighter gauge that can sometimes happen with stranding. Afterwards, use the third color yarn to add leaves with duplicate stitch. The sample features the last tree in the forest to bare leaves, but you can add leaves to as many trees as you like using a variety of colors.

2x2 Ribbing (in the round over a multiple of 4 sts)
Round 1: (P1, K2, P1) to end.
Rep this rnd to make pattern.

Stockinette Stitch (St st, in the round over any number of sts)
Round 1: K to end.
Rep this rnd to make pattern.

DIRECTIONS

Hat

The hat is worked in the round from the brim to the crown. Read each chart row from right to left.

Brim

With C1 and smaller needles CO 144 (160, 176) sts and join in the rnd being careful not to twist. PM to mark start of rnd. Work 15 rnds 2x2 Ribbing.
Inc Rnd: *K18 (20, 22), inc 1; rep from * to end - 152 (168, 184) sts.

Main Section

Switch to MC. Knit 3 rnds. Switch to larger needles.
Work Trees Chart Rows 1 through 25 - the 8 sts of each row are repeated across each rnd 19 (21, 23) times.
Switch to smaller needles. Work in St st until hat measures 7.5 (7.5, 7.75)" from CO edge.

Crown

Size 23.5 Only:
Rnd 1: (K21, K2tog) to end – 176 sts.
Rnds 2, 3, 5 & 6: K to end.
Rnd 4: (K20, K2tog) to end – 168 sts.

Sizes 21.25 & 23.5:
Rnd 7: (K19, K2tog) to end – 160 sts.
Rnds 8, 9, 11 & 12: K to end.
Rnd 10: (K18, K2tog) to end – 152 sts.

All Sizes:
Rnd 13: (K17, K2tog) to end – 144 sts.
Rnds 14, 16, 18, 20, 22, 24, 26, 28 & 30: K to end.
Rnd 15: (K16, K2tog) to end – 136 sts.
Rnd 17: (K15, K2tog) to end – 128 sts.
Rnd 19: (K14, K2tog) to end – 120 sts.
Rnd 21: (K13, K2tog) to end – 112 sts.
Rnd 23: (K12, K2tog) to end – 104 sts.
Rnd 25: (K11, K2tog) to end – 96 sts.
Rnd 27: (K10, K2tog) to end – 88 sts.
Rnd 29: (K9, K2tog) to end – 80 sts.
Rnd 31: (K8, K2tog) to end – 72 sts.
Rnd 32: (K7, K2tog) to end – 64 sts.
Rnd 33: (K6, K2tog) to end – 56 sts.
Rnd 34: (K5, K2tog) to end – 48 sts.
Rnd 35: (K4, K2tog) to end – 40 sts.
Rnd 36: (K3, K2tog) to end – 32 sts.
Rnd 37: (K2, K2tog) to end – 24 sts.
Rnd 38: (K1, K2tog) to end – 16 sts.
Rnd 39: (K2tog) to end – 8 sts.
Cut yarn leaving an 8" tail. Pull yarn tail through remaining sts, cinch and secure to close crown.

Finishing

Using C2, duplicate stitch leaves onto one of the tree motifs (top row on the side of the hat opposite the start of round) as shown in the Tree Leaves Chart.

Using C2, make a large pom-pom and secure it to the top of the hat.

Weave in ends, wash and block to finished measurements.

Tree Leaves Chart

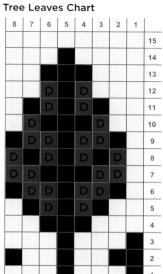

Legend

☐	**knit** knit stitch
☐	**MC**
■	**C1**
⬛ D	**Duplicate Stitch with C2**

Trees Chart

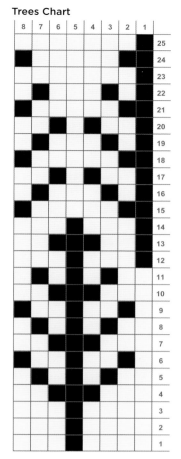

MORANA MITTENS

by Irina Anikeeva

FINISHED MEASUREMENTS

Adult S/M (L): 7 (8.5)" circumference x
10.5" from cuff to tip

YARN

Knit Picks City Tweed Aran/HW (55%
Merino Wool, 25% Superfine Alpaca, 20%
Donegal Tweed; 164 yards/100g): Jacquard
24524, 1 ball

NEEDLES

US 6 (4mm) DPNs, or size to obtain
gauge

NOTIONS

Yarn Needle
Stitch Markers
Cable Needle
Scrap yarn or stitch holder

GAUGE

18 sts and 24 rows = 4" over St st in the
round, blocked

Morana Mittens

Notes:

These mittens are worked from cuff up in the round.

All rounds on chart are read from right to left.

Make 1 Purl Stitch (M1P): With LH needle tip, pick up the thread between sts from front to back. P lifted loop TBL.

Backwards-Loop Cast On Method

Place the working yarn over your thumb. The RH needle goes under the yarn at the base of your thumb and over the yarn at the top of your thumb. Tighten your newly cast on st.

DIRECTIONS

Left Mitten

CO 34 (38) sts. PM and join in rnd, being careful not to twist sts.

Ribbing Rnd: (K1 TBL, P1) to the end of rnd.

Rep Ribbing Rnd until piece measures 3".

Pattern Set-up Rnd 1: Work Row 1 of Leaves Chart over 13 sts, PM, P to end.

Pattern Set-up Rnd 2: Work Row 2 of Leaves Chart over 13 sts, SM, P to end.

Work in pattern as established until Row 5 of Leaves Chart is complete. 36 (40) sts.

Shape Thumb Gusset

Inc Rnd 1: Work Row 6 of Leaves Chart, SM, P to last 5 (6) sts, PM, M1P, P1, M1P, PM, P to end. 2 gusset sts inc. 42 (46) sts.

Work next 2 rnds even in pattern.

Inc Rnd 2: Work next row of Leaves Chart, SM, P to M, SM, M1P, P to M, M1P, SM, P to end. 2 gusset sts inc.

Work next 2 rnds even in pattern.

Rep last 3 rnds 2 more times – 46 (50) sts.

Rep Inc Rnd 2 one more time – 46 (50) sts.

Work one more rnd (chart Rnd 19) on all sts in pattern.

Size L Only:

Rep Inc Rnd one more time – 56 sts. Work one more rnd on all sts in pattern.

At the completion of the thumb gusset increases, Row 19 (21) of Leaves Chart has been completed.

Next Rnd: Work Row 20 (22) of Leaves Chart, SM, P to M, remove M, place the 11 (13) gusset sts on scrap yarn, using Backward-Loop method, CO 1 st, remove M, P to end – 40 (46) sts.

Work in pattern on all sts, working Rows 21 (23) through Row 42 of Leaves Chart – 34 (38) sts.

P all sts for next 2 (3) rows.

Top Shaping

Dec Rnd 1: *P1, P2tog; repeat from * to last st, P1 (2) – 23 (26) sts.

Next Rnd: P.

Dec Rnd 2: *P2tog, P1; repeat from * to last 2 sts, P2tog – 15 (17) sts.

Next Rnd: P.

Dec Rnd 3: *P1, P2tog; repeat from * to end (to last 2 sts, P2tog) – 10 (11) sts.

Dec Rnd 4: *P2tog; repeat from * to end (to last st, P1) – 5 (6) sts.

Cut yarn, leaving a long tail. Pull through remaining sts, draw up and secure.

Thumb

Sl 11 (13) held sts from scrap yarn back on needle and PU 1 st from gap between CO and gusset sts, 1 st along CO st, 1 st from gap between gusset and CO sts – 14 (16) sts. PM for beginning of the rnd.

P all sts for 12 rnds.

Dec Rnd 1: *P1, P2tog; repeat from * to last 2 (1) st(s), P2tog (P1) – 9 (11) sts.

Next Rnd: P.

Dec Rnd 2: *P2tog; repeat from * to last st, P1 – 5 (6) sts.

Cut yarn, leaving a long tail. Pull through remaining sts, draw up and secure.

Right Mitten

Work as for Left Mitten to thumb gusset.

Shape Thumb Gusset

Inc Rnd: Work Row 6 of Leaves Chart, SM, P4 (5), PM, M1P, P1, M1P, PM, P to end – 2 gusset sts inc.

Continue as for Left Mitten.

Finishing

Weave in yarn ends. Block to finished measurements.

Leaves Chart

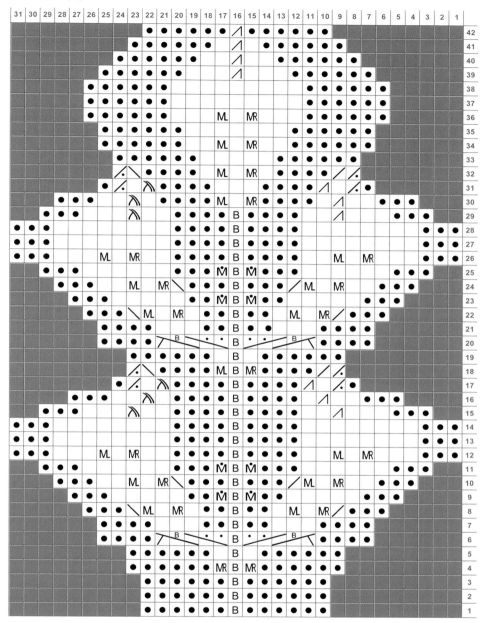

Legend

No Stitch
Placeholder - No stitch made.

purl
purl stitch

knit tbl
Knit stitch through back loop

make one right
With LH needle tip, PU the thread between sts from back to front. Knit lifted loop through front loop

knit
knit stitch

Right Leaf Increase
slip 2 sts onto CN and hold in back, increase 2 sts (K1 TBL and then to front loop) in the same stitch. Insert LH needle behind the vertical strand that runs downward between 2 sts just made and K1TBL into this strand to make the 3rd st. Purl 2 sts from CN

Left Leaf Increase
slip 1 st onto CN and hold in front, purl 2 sts. Increase 2 sts (K1 TBL and then to front loop in the same stitch. Insert LH needle behind the vertical strand that runs downward between 2 sts just made and K1TBL into this strand to make the 3rd st). Purl 2 sts from CN

k2tog
Knit two stitches together as one stitch

make one left
With LHneedle tip, PU the thread between sts from front to back. Knit lifted loop TBL

ssk
Slip one stitch as if to knit, Slip another stitch as if to knit. Insert left-hand needle into front of these 2 stitches and knit them together

make one purl
With LH needle tip, PU thread between sts from front to back. Purl lifted loop TBL

k3tog
Knit three stitches together as one

sssk
(Slip 1 as if to knit) 3 times; insert left-hand needle from the front to the back of all stitches at the same time and knit them together.

p2tog
Purl 2 stitches together

NORTHERN SHORES COWL

by Jennifer Chase-Rappaport

FINISHED MEASUREMENTS

8″ depth at deepest point in lace pattern x 22″ circumference

YARN

Knit Picks Biggo (50% Superwash Merino Wool, 50% Nylon; 110 yards/100g): Sapphire Heather 25626, 1 hank

NEEDLES

US 10.5 (6.5mm) straight or circular needles, or size to obtain gauge

NOTIONS

Yarn Needle

Scrap yarn (optional for provisional cast-on)

Size H Crochet hook or larger (optional for provisional cast-on)

Spare circular needle same size or smaller than needle used for knitting

GAUGE

12 sts and 18 rows = 4″ over lace pattern, blocked. (Gauge for this project is approximate)

Northern Shores Cowl

Notes:

Northern Shores Cowl is a cozy neckwarmer inspired by winter walks on the beach. Using just one skein of Knit Picks' Biggo, it is a quick knit perfect for gifting or treating yourself. The cowl is knit flat lengthwise and the ends are grafted together at finishing. For best results, a provisional cast-on is recommended to make the joining as invisible as possible. A link to a tutorial for this technique is provided below. Advice is given in the finishing section for knitters who prefer not to use a provisional cast-on. Stitch counts change on some rows of the lace pattern. On rows where this happens, the correct stitch count is indicated at the end of the row. When working the chart, follow RS rows (even numbers) from right to left, and WS rows (odd numbers) from left to right.

Provisional Cast-on

A provisional cast-on is recommended for this cowl to make grafting the ends of the project as smooth as possible. A useful video for my preferred technique can be found here: http://tutorials.knitpicks.com/wptutorials/crocheted-provisional-cast-on/ .

DIRECTIONS

Using your preferred cast-on (please see Notes above), CO 22 sts. Using either written instructions below or Chart, work Rows 1-14 seven times total. Cut yarn leaving a 36" tail attached to the work for grafting.

Row 1 and all WS rows through Row 13: K2, P to last 3 sts, K3.

Row 2 (RS): Sl 1 P-wise WYIF, K12, YO, K5, YO, Ssk, YO, K2. (24 sts)

Row 4: Sl 1 P-wise WYIF, K13, Sk2p, K2, (YO, K2tog) twice, K1. (22 sts)

Row 6: Sl 1 P-wise WYIF, K12, Ssk, K2, (YO, K2tog) twice, K1. (21 sts)

Row 8: Sl 1 P-wise WYIF, K11, Ssk, K2, (YO, K2tog) twice, K1. (20 sts)

Row 10: Sl 1 P-wise WYIF, K10, Ssk, K2, (YO, K2tog) twice, K1. (19 sts)

Row 12: Sl 1 P-wise WYIF, K9, Ssk, K2, YO, K1, YO, Ssk, YO, K2. (20 sts)

Row 14: Sl 1 P-wise WYIF, K12, YO, K3, YO, Ssk, YO, K2. (22 sts)

Finishing

If a provisional CO was used, remove waste yarn and place live sts on a spare needle. With RS facing, graft ends of piece together. If a regular CO was used, place live sts on circular needle and graft to the base of the corresponding sts in the CO row. A tutorial for Kitchener Stitch can be found on Knit Picks' web site here: http://tutorials.knitpicks.com/wptutorials/kitchener-stitch/ Weave in ends, wash and block to measurements, pinning out points of lace edge for best definition.

Northern Shores Chart

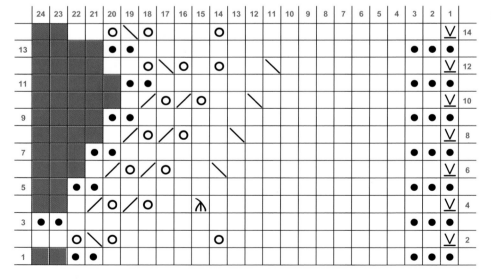

Legend

●	**purl**	RS: purl stitch / WS: knit stitch
☐	**knit**	RS: knit stitch / WS: purl stitch
V	**slip 1 P-wise WYIF**	Slip stitch as if to purl, with yarn held in front
O	**yo**	yarn over
◣	**ssk**	Slip one stitch as if to knit, Slip another stitch as if to knit. Insert left-hand needle into front of these 2 stitches and knit them together
⋀	**Sk2p**	Slip 1, k2tog, pass slipped stitch over k2tog
◢	**k2tog**	Knit two stitches together as one stitch
▓	**No Stitch**	Placeholder - No stitch made.

POSIE BONNET

by Lynnette Hulse

FINISHED MEASUREMENTS

To fit size newborn (baby, toddler, child) with 12 (14, 16, 18)" head circumference. 5.5 (6, 6.5, 7)" deep x 6 (6.5, 7.25, 7.75)" tall at brim, blocked and measured flat. Item is meant to be worn fitted with a small amount of negative ease

YARN

Knit Picks Swish Worsted (100% Superwash Merino Wool; 110 yards/50g): Hollyberry 25148, 1 (1, 1, 2) ball(s)

NEEDLES

US 8 (5mm) straight or circular needles plus 2 DPNs, or size to obtain gauge

NOTIONS

Yarn Needle
Stitch Markers
Cable Needle

GAUGE

26 sts and 36 rows = 4" Slipped Double Cable pattern, blocked
19 sts and 29 rows = 4" in St st, blocked. (Gauge for this project is approximate)

Posie Bonnet

Notes:

Posie Bonnet is worked flat in two directions, then seamlessly joined at the center back with Kitchener stitch. DPNs or similar needles are required for the attached Icord and ties.

Read the chart from right to left on RS rows (odd numbers), and left to right on WS rows (even numbers).

Slip stitches purlwise.

Slipped Double Cable Chart (worked flat over 16 sts)

Row 1 (RS): SL1, K4, SL1, P4, K2, SL2, K2.
Row 2 (WS): P2, SL1WYIF twice, P2, K4, SL1WYIF, P4, SL1WYIF.
Row 3 - 4: Repeat Rows 1 - 2.
Row 5: 1/2 LC, 1/2 RC, P4, 1/2 RC, 1/2 LC.
Row 6: P6, K4, P6.
Repeat Rows 1-6 for pattern.

1/2 LC

SL1 st to CN, hold to front of work, K2, K1 from CN.

1/2 RC

SL2 sts to CN, hold to back of work. K1, K2 from CN.

Right Lifted Increase (RLI)

With the working needle, lift the st below the next st onto the left hand needle, knit that stitch.

I-cord

*Knit a row. Slide row to other end of needle without turning work. Pull yarn firmly and repeat from *, creating a tube.

Attached I-cord

With RS of bonnet facing you, PU one st from under CO edge onto left side needle. K2TOG, K2. Slide sts to the right end of the needle as with normal Icord and repeat.

DIRECTIONS

Brim

CO 26 sts.

Slip markers as you come to them.

Row 1 (RS): P6, PM, K6, PM, P4, PM, K6, PM, P3, SL1WYIF.
Row 2 (WS): K4, P6, K4, P6, K5, SL1.
Row 3: P6, work Slipped Double Cable Chart, P3, SL1WYIF.
Row 4: K4, work Slipped Double Cable Chart, K5, SL1.
Row 5: Repeat Rows 3 & 4 until 14 (16, 18, 20) repeats of Slipped Double Cable Chart are complete.
Row 6: P6, K6, P4, K6, P3, SL1WYIF.
Row 7: Repeat Row 2.

BO 26 sts. Do not break yarn or pull through final st, 1 st remains on right hand needle.

Back & Pixie Point

Turn work 90 degrees and PU & K 43 (49, 55, 61) sts. (44, 50, 56, 62 sts)

Row 1 (WS): P22 (25, 27, 30), PM, P to 1 st before end, SL1 WYIF.
Rows 2 & 3 for sizes 6, 6.5, 7"/ 15.25, 16.5, 18 cm ONLY:
Row 2 (RS): K to 1st before end, SL1.
Row 3: P to 1st before end, SL1WYIF.
Repeat Rows 2 & 3 0 (1, 2, 3, 4) more times, ending with a WS row.

All Sizes:
Row 4 (RS): K to 2sts before M, (RLI, K1) four times, K to 1 st before end, SL1. 4 sts inc.
Row 5: P to 1st before end, SL1 WYIF.

Repeat Rows 4 & 5 3 times. 56 (62, 68, 74) sts.

Break yarn leaving a long tail (approximately three times the width of the work). Distribute work across two needles evenly and Kitchener closed using long tail.

Ties

CO 3 sts onto a DPN and work Icord for 11 (12, 13, 14)"/ 28 (30.5, 33, 35.5) cm. Join to base of bonnet and work around base in Attached Icord. Continue Icord for another 11 (12, 13, 14)"/ 28 (30.5, 33, 35.5) cm to match the first string. Cut yarn, pull tail through sts to fasten off.

Finishing

Weave in all ends, gently block to dimensions, allowing front edge to curl back, forming a rolled brim that matches the look of the Icord.

Slipped Double Cable

	16	15	14	13	12	11	10	9	8	7	6	5	4	3	2	1	
6							●	●	●	●							
	1/2 LC / 1/2 RC (cols 16–11)										1/2 LC / 1/2 RC (cols 6–1)						5
4			V	V			●	●	●	●	V					V	
			V	V			●	●	●	●	V					V	3
2			V	V			●	●	●	●	V					V	
			V	V			●	●	●	●	V					V	1

Legend

slip
RS: Slip stitch as if to purl, holding yarn in back
WS: Slip stitch as if to purl, holding yarn in front
(symbol: V)

knit
RS: knit stitch
WS: purl stitch
(symbol: empty box)

purl
RS: purl stitch
WS: knit stitch
(symbol: ●)

1/2 LC
sl 1 to CN, hold in front. k2, k1 from CN

1/2 RC
sl2 to CN, hold in back. k1, k2 from CN

DOUBLE LEAF COWL

by Quenna Lee

FINISHED MEASUREMENTS
45" circumference x 7.25" high

YARN
Knit Picks Preciosa Tonal Worsted (100% Merino Wool; 273 yards/100g): Bonsai 26719, 2 hanks

NEEDLES
US 9 (5.5mm) 24" circular needle, or size to obtain gauge

NOTIONS
Yarn Needle
Stitch Markers

GAUGE
17 sts and 28 rnds = 4" in St st, blocked
6" across x 3" high = One rep of Lace and Mock Cable pattern, blocked

Double Leaf Cowl

Notes:

This cowl is worked in the round from the bottom up. The Lace Pattern and Mock Cable can be worked from charts or text. When using the charts, read each row from right to left.

Lace Pattern (in the rnd over multiples of 17 sts)
Rnd 1: K2, YO, K3tog, YO, K1, K2tog, YO, K1, YO, SSK, K1, YO, SSSK, YO, K2.
Rnds 2, 4, 6, 8: K.
Rnd 3: K1, YO, K3tog, YO, K1, K2tog, (K1, YO) x 2, K1, SSK, K1, YO, SSSK, YO, K1.
Rnd 5: YO, K3tog, YO, K1, K2tog, K2, YO, K1, YO, K2, SSK, K1, YO, SSSK, YO.
Rnd 7: YO, CDD, YO, K1, YO, SSK, K5, K2tog, YO, K1, YO, CDD, YO.
Rnd 9: K1, YO, SSK, K2, YO, SSK, K3, K2tog, YO, K2, K2tog, YO, K1.
Rnd 10: K1, P1, K13, P1, K1.
Rnd 11: K1, P1, YO, SSSK, YO, K1, YO, SSK, K1, K2tog, YO, K1, YO, K3tog, YO, P1, K1.
Rnd 12: Rep Rnd 10.
Rnd 13: K1, P1, K1, YO, SSK, K2, YO, SSSK, YO, K2, K2tog, YO, K1, P1, K1.
Rnd 14: (K1, P1) x 2, K9, (P1, K1) x 2.
Rnd 15: (K1, P1) x 2, YO, SSSK, YO, K3, YO, K3tog, YO, (P1, K1) x 2.
Rnd 16: Rep Rnd 14.
Rnd 17: (K1, P1) x 2, K1, YO, SSK, YO, SSSK, YO, K2tog, YO, (K1, P1) x 2, K1.
Rnds 18, 20, 22: (K1, P1) x 3, K5, (P1, K1) x 3.
Rnd 19: (K1, P1) x 3, YO, SSK, K1, K2tog, YO, (P1, K1) x 3.
Rnd 21: (K1, P1) x 3, K1, YO, SSSK, YO, (K1, P1) x 3, K1.
Rep Rnds 1-22 for pattern.

Mock Cable (in the rnd over 5 sts)
Rnd 1: P1, SL 3rd st over 1st 2 sts; K1, YO, K1, P1.
Rnds 2-4: P1, K3, P1.
Rep Rnds 1-4 for pattern.

Center Double Decrease (CDD): SL 2 sts P-wise, K1, pass slipped sts over.
1/2 RC: SL 2 sts to CN, place in back, K1, K2 from CN.

DIRECTIONS

CO 198 sts. PM, join for working in the rnd being careful not to twist sts.

Bottom Edging
Rnd 1: *K39, PM, P1, K3, P1, (K1, P1) x 3, K5, (P1, K1) x 3, P1, K3, P1, PM, rep from * twice more.
Rnd 2: *P7, (K1, P7) x 4, SM, work pattern as established to M, SM, rep from * twice more.

Rep Rnds 1-2 once more.

Body
Next Rnd: *Work in pattern to M, SM, work Mock Cable pattern over 5 sts, work Leaf pattern over 17 sts, work Mock Cable pattern over 5 sts, SM, rep from * twice more.

Work as established until Rnds 1-22 of Leaf pattern are worked twice.

Top Edging
Rnd 1: *Work in pattern to M, SM, P1, 1/2 RC, P1, (K1, P1) x 3, K5, (P1, K1) x 3, P1, 1/2 RC, P1, SM, rep from * twice more.
Rnds 2-3: *Work in pattern to M, SM, P1, K3, P1, (K1, P1) x 3, K5, (P1, K1) x 3, P1, K3, P1, SM, rep from * twice more.

BO loosely in pattern.

Finishing
Weave in ends, wash and block to size.

Leaf Chart

17	16	15	14	13	12	11	10	9	8	7	6	5	4	3	2	1	
	●		●		●						●		●		●		22
	●		●		●	O	/	Λ	O		●		●		●		21
	●		●		●						●		●		●		20
	●		●		●	O	/		\	O	●		●		●		19
	●		●		●						●		●		●		18
	●		●		O	/	O	Λ	O	\	O		●		●		17
	●		●										●		●		16
	●	O	/	O				O	Λ	O		●	●		●		15
	●		●										●				14
	●	O	/			O	Λ	O			\	O		●		●	13
	●															●	12
	●	O	/	O		O	/		\	O		O	Λ	O	●		11
	●															●	10
	O	/			O	/				\	O			\	O		9
																	8
O	Λ	O		O	/				\	O		O	Λ	O			7
																	6
O	Λ	O		\			O		O			/		O	/	O	5
																	4
	O	Λ	O		\		O		O		/		O	/	O		3
																	2
	O	Λ	O			\	O		O	/		O	/	O			1

Legend

- **knit** — knit stitch (□)
- **yo** — Yarn Over (O)
- **k3tog** — Knit three stitches together as one (⟋ in box)
- **k2tog** — Knit two stitches together as one stitch (/)
- **ssk** — Slip one stitch as if to knit, Slip another stitch as if to knit. Insert left-hand needle into front of these 2 stitches and knit them together (\)
- **sssk** — Slip 3 sts as if to knit. Insert needle from the front to the back of all stitches at the same time and knit them together (Λ)
- **Central Double Dec** — Slip first and second stitches together as if to knit. Knit 1 stitch. Pass two slipped stitches over the knit stitch. (Λ)
- **purl** — purl stitch (●)
- **Mock Cable Stitch** — Sl 3rd st over first 2 sts; K1, YO, K1

Mock Cable Chart

	5	4	3	2	1	
4	●				●	
	●				●	3
2	●				●	
	●	⌐— O ⌐ (Mock Cable Stitch)			●	1

RUNNER HAT

by Stana D. Sortor

FINISHED MEASUREMENTS
16.5 (18.5, 20.5)" circumference x 8.25 (9.5, 11)" high

YARN
Knit Picks Swish DK (100% Superwash Merino Wool; 123 yards/50g): MC Cobblestone Heather 24313, C1 Dove Heather 24956, 1 ball each

NEEDLE
US 5 (3.75mm) DPNs or circular needles, or size to obtain gauge
US 4 (3.5mm) DPNs or circular needles, or one size smaller than needle used to obtain gauge

NOTIONS
Yarn Needle
Stitch Markers

GAUGE
22 sts and 34 rows = 4" in Slipped Stitch Pattern on larger needles in the round, blocked

Runner Hat

Notes:

This hat is knitted in the round. The brim is worked in 2 x 2 Ribbing. The main body is worked in a slipped stitch pattern, working with just one color of yarn each round.

2 x 2 Rib (in the round over multiples of 4 sts)
All Rounds: *K2, P2; repeat from * to the end of round.

Slipped Stitch Pattern (in the round over multiples of 4 sts)
Round 1: *Sl 1, K3 in C1; repeat from * to the end of round.
Round 2: K2 in MC, *Sl 1, K3 in MC; repeat until last 2 sts , Sl 1, K1 in MC.
Rep Rounds 1 – 2 for pattern.

DIRECTIONS
Brim
Using smaller needle and C1 loosely CO 88 (100, 112) sts. PM, being careful not to twist sts, join to begin working in the round.
Rounds 1 - 10: Work in 2 x 2 Rib in C1. Attach MC.
Rounds 11 - 20: Work in 2 x 2 Rib in MC.

Body
Switch to larger needle.
Round 21: Knit around in MC.
Work in Slipped Stitch Pattern for 40 (50, 60) rounds.

Crown
Decrease Rounds – Size 16" only:
Round 1: Sl 1, K3tog in C1, (Sl 1, K3 in C1) 8x, Sl 1, K3tog in C1, (Sl 1, K3 in C1) 12x. (84 sts)
Round 2: K3tog in MC, K1 in MC, (Sl 1, K3 in MC) 7x, Sl 1, K1 in MC, K3tog in MC, K1 in MC, (Sl 1, K3 in MC) 11x, Sl 1, K1 in MC. (80 sts)

Decrease Rounds – Size 18.5" only:
Round 1: *Sl 1, K3tog in C1, (Sl 1, K3 in C1) 4x; rep from * 5x. (90 sts)
Round 2: *K3tog in MC, K1 in MC, (Sl 1, K3 in MC) 3x, Sl 1, K1 in MC; rep from * 5x. (80 sts)

Decrease Rounds – Size 20.5" only:
Round 1: Sl 1, K3tog in C1, (Sl 1, K3 in C1) 10x, Sl 1, K3tog in C1, (Sl 1, K3 in C1) 5x, Sl 1, K3tog in C1, (Sl 1, K3 in C1) 10x. (106 sts)
Round 2: K3tog in MC, K1 in MC, (Sl 1, K3 in MC) 9x, Sl 1, K1 in MC, K3tog in MC, K1 in MC, (Sl 1, K3 in MC) 4x, Sl 1, K1 in MC, K3tog in MC, K1 in MC, (Sl 1, K3 in MC) 9x, Sl 1, K1 in MC. (100 sts)
Round 3: *Sl 1, K3tog in C1, (Sl 1, K3 in C1) 4x; rep from * 5x. (90 sts)
Round 4: *K3tog in MC, K1 in MC, (Sl 1, K3 in MC) 3x, Sl 1, K1 in MC; rep from * 5x. (80 sts)

Final Decrease Rounds – All Sizes:
Round 1: *Sl 1, K3tog in C1, (Sl 1, K3 in C1) 3x; rep from * 5x. (70 sts)
Round 2: *K3tog in MC, K1 in MC, (Sl 1, K3 in MC) 2x, Sl 1, K1 in MC; rep from * 5x. (60 sts)
Round 3: *Sl 1, K3tog in C1, (Sl 1, K3 in C1) 2x; rep from * 5x. (50 sts)
Round 4: *K3tog in MC, K1 in MC, Sl 1, K3 in MC, Sl 1, K1 in MC; rep from * 5x. (40 sts)
Round 5: *Sl 1, K3tog in C1, Sl 1, K3 in C1; rep from * 5x. (30 sts)
Round 6: *K3tog in MC, K1 in MC, Sl 1, K1 in MC; rep from * 5x. (20 sts)
Round 7: *Sl 1, K3tog in C1; rep from * 5x. (10 sts). Cut off C1.
Round 8: *K2tog in MC; rep from * 5x. (5 sts)

Cut the yarn, leaving long tail, and thread the end on a yarn needle. Pull the end through the remaining sts on needles, gather up and close the hole, stitch to secure.

Finishing
Weave in ends, wash and block to measurements.

SNOWY BUNNY

by Emily Kintigh

FINISHED MEASUREMENTS

Approximately 15" tall and 11" around the middle

YARN

Knit Picks Biggo (50% Superwash Merino Wool, 50% Nylon; 110 yards/100g): MC Bare 26089, 2 balls
Knit Picks Swish Worsted (100% Superwash Merino Wool; 110 yards/50g): C1 Dove Heather 25631, 1 ball, or scrap yarn for embroidery

NEEDLES

US 10 (6mm) DPNs or two 24" circular needles for two circulars technique, or one 32" or longer circular needle for Magic Loop technique, or size to obtain gauge

NOTIONS

Yarn Needle
Stitch Markers
Pom-pom maker for 2.5" pom-pom
Stuffing

GAUGE

15 sts and 21 rows = 4" in St st in the round, blocked.

Snowy Bunny

Notes:

The head, body, arms, and legs are all worked in the round. The ears are worked flat. Short rows are used to form the heels of the feet. Work in MC for entire bunny except embroidery.

DIRECTIONS

Head

Loosely CO 6 sts. PM and join in the rnd being careful not to twist the sts.

Rnds 1, 3, 5, 7: K to end.
Rnd 2: KFB to end. 12 sts.
Rnd 4: (K2, M1) to end. 18 sts.
Rnd 6: (K3, M1) to end. 24 sts.
Rnd 8: (K4, M1) to end. 30 sts.
Rnds 9-18: K to end.

Weave in CO end closing up the hole at the CO edge.

Rnd 19: (SSK, K6, K2tog) to end. 24 sts.
Rnd 20: K to end.
Rnd 21: (SSK, K4, K2tog) to end. 18 sts.
Rnd 20-24: K to end. Add stuffing.
Rnd 25: (SSK, K2, K2tog) to end. 12 sts.
Rnd 26: (SSK, K2tog) to end. 6 sts.

Add last bit of stuffing. Cut yarn and pull through remaining sts.

Body

Loosely CO 18 sts, leaving a long tail to sew the head to the body with. PM and join in the rnd being careful not to twist the sts.

Rnd 1: (K1, P1) to end.
Rnd 2: (P1, K1) to end.
Rnd 3: Repeat Rnd 1.
Rnd 4: (P1, K1, KFB, K1, P1, KFB) to end. 24 sts.
Rnd 5: *(K1, P1) twice, (P1, K1) twice; rep from * to end.
Rnd 6: *(P1, K1) twice, (K1, P1) twice; rep from * to end.
Rnd 7: Repeat Rnd 5.
Rnd 8: (P1, K1, P1, KFB, K1, P1, K1, KFB) to end. 30 sts.
Rnds 9- 28: Repeat Rnds 1-2.
Rnd 29: (K1, P1, K1, K2tog, P1, K1, P1, P2tog) to end. 24 sts.
Rnd 30: (P1, K1, P2, K1, P1, K2) to end.
Rnd 31: (K1, P1, K2tog, P1, K1, P2tog) to end. 18 sts.
Rnd 32: Repeat Rnd 2.
Rnd 33: (K2tog, P2tog, K2tog) to end. 9 sts.

Cut yarn and pull through remaining sts.

Arm (make two)

Loosely CO 12 sts, leaving a long tail to sew the arm to the body with. PM and join in the rnd being careful not to twist the sts.

Rnds 1-20: K to end.
Rnd 21: K2tog to end. 6 sts.
Cut yarn and pull through remaining sts.

Leg (make two)

Loosely CO 12 sts. PM and join in the rnd being careful not to twist the sts.

Rnds 1-25: K to end.

Short Row Heel

The heel shaping is formed by using short rows with wraps and turns. Make sure to pick up and work all wraps when working a previously wrapped st.

Row 1: K10, W&T.
Row 2: P8, W&T.
Row 3: K7, W&T.
Row 4: P6, W&T.
Row 5: K5, W&T.
Row 6: P4, W&T.
Row 7: Repeat Row 5.
Row 8: Repeat Row 4.
Row 9: Repeat Row 3.
Row 10: Repeat Row 2.
Row 11: K to end.

Foot

Continue working in the round, picking up the last wraps from the heel shaping on the second st of the first rnd.

Rnds 1-10: K to end.
Rnd 11: K2tog to end. 6 sts.

Cut yarn and pull through remaining sts.

Ear (make two)

Loosely CO 5 sts, leaving a long tail to sew the ear to the head with.

Row 1: (K1, P1) to last st, K1.
Row 2: KFB, P1, K1, P1, KFB. 7 sts.
Row 3: (P1, K1) to last st, P1.
Row 4: KFB, (K1, P1) twice, K1, KFB. 9 sts.
Row 5: (K1, P1) to last st, K1.
Rows 6-29: Repeat Row 5.
Row 30: P2tog, (K1, P1) twice, K1, P2tog. 7 sts.
Rows 31-33: Repeat Row 3.
Row 34: K2tog, P1, K1, P1, K2tog. 5 sts.
Rows 35-37: Repeat Row 5.
Row 38: P2tog, K1, P2tog. 3 sts.
Row 39: P1, K1, P1.

Cut yarn and pull through remaining sts.

Finishing

Add stuffing to the body and then sew the body to the head making sure that the Y shape formed by the decreases at the front of the head is upright. Stuff arms and legs and sew securely them to the body. Sew the ears to the top of the head. Using the pom-pom maker, make the tail and then sew the tail to the body. With C1 or scrap yarn, embroider the nose, using the decreases from the head as a guide. Embroider the mouth and eyes as pictured. Weave in any remaining ends.

STRUCTURED SLIPPERS

by Mone Dräger

FINISHED MEASUREMENTS

S (M, L), foot circumference 7 (8, 9)" x foot length 9 (10, 11)"

YARN

Knit Picks Swish Worsted (100% Superwash Merino wool; 110 yards/50g): Lost Lake Heather 25146, 2 (2, 3) balls

NEEDLES

US 6 (4mm) DPNs or two 24" circular needles for two circulars technique, or one 32" or longer circular needle for Magic Loop technique, or size to obtain gauge

NOTIONS

Yarn Needle
Stitch Markers

GAUGE

24 sts and 30 rows = 4" over Double Moss Stitch in the rnd, blocked

Structured Slippers

Notes:

The slippers are knit in modules that are joined while knitting. Some parts of the pattern (the cuff, increase section and the transition to the sole) are worked in the round, some parts of the pattern (the instep and the sole) are worked flat. The toe shaping is done using German short rows with double stitches.

Structured Pattern (in the round over multiples of 6 sts)
Round 1: *Sl1, YO, K1, PSSO, P1, K2, P1; rep from * to end of rnd.
Round 2 and all even numbered rounds: *K2, P1, K2, P1; rep from * to end of rnd.
Rounds 3-8: Rep Rounds 1-2 three more times.
Round 9: *K2, P1, Sl1, YO, K1, PSSO, P1; rep from * to end of rnd.
Round 10: Rep Round 2.
Rounds 11-16: Rep Rounds 9-10 three more times.

Structured Pattern (worked flat over multiples of 6 sts)
Row 1 (RS): *Sl1, YO, K1, PSSO, P1, K2, P1; rep from * to end of row.
Row 2 and all even numbered rows (WS): *K1, P2, K1, P2; rep from * to end of row.
Rows 3-8: Rep Rows 1-2 three more times.
Row 9: *K2, P1, Sl1, YO, K1, PSSO, P1; rep from * to end of row.
Row 10: Rep Row 2.
Rows 11-16: Rep Rows 9-10 three more times.

Double Moss Stitch (in the round over an even number of sts)
Rnd 1: *K1, P1; rep from * to end of rnd.
Rnd 2: *P1, K1; rep from * to end of rnd.
Rnd 3: Rep Rnd 2.
Rnd 4: Rep Rnd 1.
Rep Rnds 1-4 for pattern.

Double Stitch (DS)
Bring the working yarn in front, Sl the next st P-wise, bring the working yarn from front to back over the needle and pull on it enough to bring the legs of that st over the needle. The st on the needle looks like a double st. When working the DS the next time, K into both legs and treat as one st.

Make 1 Stitch (M1)
PU the bar between st just worked and next st and place on LH needle as a regular stitch; K TBL. 1 st inc.

Kitchener Stitch (grafting)
With an equal number of sts on two needles, thread end of working yarn through yarn needle. Hold needles parallel with RS's facing and both needles pointing to the right. Perform Step 2 on the first front st, and then Step 4 on the first back st, and then continue with instructions below.
1. Pull yarn needle K-wise though front st and drop st from knitting needle.
2. Pull yarn needle P-wise through next front st, leave st on knitting needle.
3. Pull yarn needle P-wise through first back st and drop st from knitting needle.
4. Pull yarn needle K-wise through next back st, leave st on knitting needle.
Repeat Steps 1 – 4 until all sts have been grafted.

DIRECTIONS
Cuff (in the round)
Loosely CO 42 (48, 54) sts. Distribute sts across needles as you prefer, PM, and join to work in the round, being careful not to twist.
Set Up Rnd: *K2, P1, rep from * to end of rnd.

Work Rnds 1-16 of Structured Pattern in the Rnd.

Gusset Increase Section (in the round)
Rnd 1: *Sl1, YO, K1, PSSO, P1, K2, P1; rep from * once, M1, *K1, P1; rep from * to end of rnd, M1. 44 (50, 56) sts.
Rnd 2: (K2, P1) 4 times, M1, *P1, K1; rep from * to end of rnd, M1. 46 (52, 58) sts.
Rnd 3: *Sl1, YO, K1, PSSO, P1, K2, P1; rep from * once, M1, *P1, K1; rep from * to end of rnd, M1. 48 (54, 60) sts.
Rnd 4: (K2, P1) 4 times, M1, *K1, P1; rep from * to end of rnd, M1. 50 (56, 62) sts.
Rnds 5-7: Rep Rnds 1-3. 56 (62, 68) sts.
Rnd 8: (K2, P1) 4 times, *K1, P1; rep from * to last 2 sts, K1. The last st of the rnd stays unworked and will be used for the instep.

Instep (worked flat)
The instep is worked back and forth over the next 13 sts.
Row 1 (RS): P1, *K2, P1, Sl1, YO, K1, PSSO, P1; rep from * once, turn.
Row 2 (WS): K1, (P2, K1) 4 times, turn.
Rows 3-8: Rep Rows 1-2 three times.
Row 9: P1, *Sl1, YO, K1, PSSO, P1, K2, P1; rep from * once, turn.
Row 10: Rep Row 2.
Rows 11-16: Rep Rows 9-10 three times.
Repeat established pattern for 8 (16, 24) more rows.

Instep Toe Shaping (worked flat)
Row 1 (RS): P1, (K2, P1) 4 times, turn.
Row 2 (WS): DS, (P2, K1) 4 times, turn.
Row 3: DS, work in established pattern up to the DS worked in last row, turn.
Rep Row 3 three more times.
Next Row: DS, K3, PM for new beginning of rnd.

Transition to Sole (in the round)
To resume working in the round, sts are picked up along the edges of the instep; for each 4 rows worked, 3 sts are picked up.
Set Up Rnd: (K1, P1) 3 times, K1, PU 18 (24, 30) sts along the edge of the instep, (P1, K1) 21 (24, 27) times, P1, PU 18 (24, 30) sts along the edge of the instep, (K1, P1) three times. 92 (110, 128) sts.
Work 8 rnds of Double Moss Stitch.

Sole (worked flat)
Set-up rnd: Remove M, K39 (47, 55), PM, K15 (17, 19), PM, K35 (43, 51) (end of rnd 3 sts before end of previous rnd).
Following, the garter stitch sole is worked back and forth in rows.
Shape Toe End
Row 1 (RS): K7, K2tog, turn. 1 st dec.
Row 2 (WS): Sl1, K7, K2tog, turn. 1 st dec.
Row 3: Sl1, K to 1 st before the gap created in previous row, K2tog, K1, turn. 1 st dec.
Rep Row 3 five (seven, nine) more times. 84 (100, 110) sts; 15 (17, 19) sts between the gaps.

Center

Row 1 (RS): Sl1, K to 1 st before the gap created in previous row, Sl2 WYIF, turn.

Row 2 (WS): K2tog, K to 1 st before the gap created in previous row, K2tog, turn. 2 sts dec.

Rep last two rows until all sts before the markers have been worked, remove markers. 30 (34, 38) sts.

Shape Heel End

Row 1 (RS): Sl1, K1, K2tog, K to 4 sts before the gap created in previous row, K2tog, K1, Sl2 WYIF, turn. 2 sts dec.

Row 2 (WS): K2tog, K to 1 st before the gap created in previous row, K2tog, turn. 2 sts dec.

Rep Row 1-2 two (three, four) more times. 18 sts; 9 sts each on sole and heel.

Finishing

Graft stitches together using Kitchener stitch. Weave in ends.

VOYAGEUR SCARF

by Holli Yeoh

FINISHED MEASUREMENTS
10" wide x 67" long

YARN
Knit Picks Hawthorne Fingering (80% Superwash Fine Highland Wool 20% Polyamide (Nylon); 357 yards/100g): Irvington 26439, 2 skeins

NEEDLES
US 5 (3.75mm) straight or short circular needles, or size to obtain gauge

NOTIONS
3 Stitch Markers
Yarn Needle

GAUGE
Chart measures 9" wide and 40 rows = 4", unblocked
Chart measures 10" wide and 32 rows (2 repeats) = 4", blocked and relaxed

Voyageur Scarf

Notes:

Inspired by the ceinture fléchée, a traditional sash worn by the French Canadian voyageurs in the 19th century, this scarf features diagonal lines of lace broken up by horizontal garter stitch ridges.

Slip all stitches as if to purl, with yarn in front.

On the rows following the double yarnovers (YO2), knit into the first yarnover and purl into the second yarnover.

When working the chart, read RS rows (even numbers) from right to left, and WS rows (odd numbers) from left to right.

Follow either the written instructions or the chart.

Voyageur Chart (worked flat over 53 sts)

Row 1 (RS): SL 1 WYIF, K6, PM, K4, (K2TOG, K1, YO) 5 times, PM, K1, (YO, K1, SSK) 5 times, K4, PM, K to end of row.

Row 2 (WS): SL 1 WYIF, K to first M, P to last M, K to end.

Row 3: SL 1 WYIF, K1, K2TOG, YO2, K2TOG, K1, SM, K3, (K2TOG, K1, YO) 5 times, K3, (YO, K1, SSK) 5 times, K3, SM, K1, K2TOG, YO2, K2TOG, K2.

Row 4: SL 1 WYIF, K2, (K1, P1) into double YO, K2, P to last M, K2, (K1, P1) into double YO, K3.

Row 5: SL 1 WYIF, K1, K2TOG, YO2, K2TOG, K1, SM, K2, (K2TOG, K1, YO) 5 times, K5, (YO, K1, SSK) 5 times, K2, SM, K1, K2TOG, YO2, K2TOG, K2.

Row 6: Rep Row 4.

Row 7: SL 1 WYIF, K1, K2TOG, YO2, K2TOG, K1, SM, K1, (K2TOG, K1, YO) 5 times, K7, (YO, K1, SSK) 5 times, K1, SM, K1, K2TOG, YO2, K2TOG, K2.

Row 8: Rep Row 4.

Row 9: SL 1 WYIF, K to next M, (K2TOG, K1, YO) 5 times, K9, (YO, K1, SSK) 5 times, SM, K to end.

Row 10: Rep Row 2.

Rows 11 to 16: SL 1 WYIF, K to end.

Rep Rows 1-16 for pattern.

DIRECTIONS

Scarf

CO 53 sts.

Row 1 (RS): SL 1 WYIF, K to end.

Rep last row 9 times more.

Work Rows 1 to 16 of Voyageur Chart 33 times or until piece measures 53.5".

Next Row (RS): SL 1 WYIF, K to end.

Rep last row 3 times more. BO all sts.

Finishing

Weave in ends. Block to 11" wide and 70" long. Scarf will relax to finished measurements after blocking.

Voyageur Chart

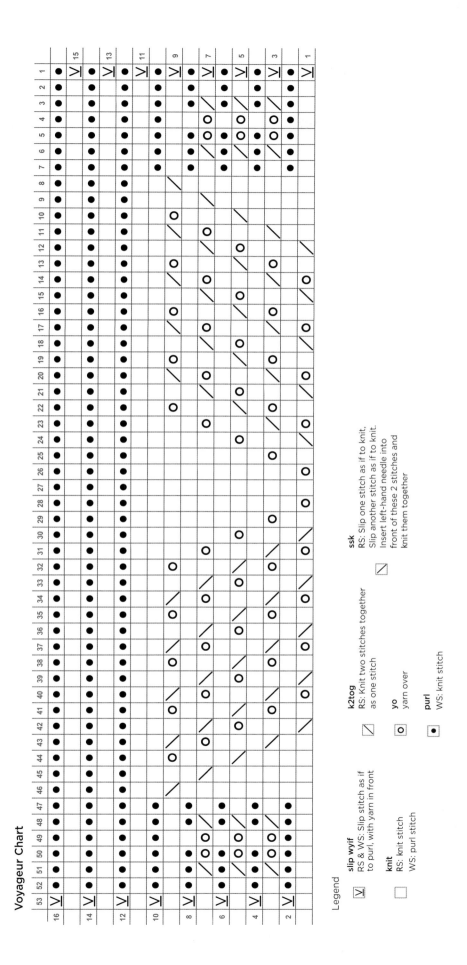

Legend

slip wyif
RS & WS: Slip stitch as if to purl, with yarn in front

knit
RS: knit stitch
WS: purl stitch

k2tog
RS: Knit two stitches together as one stitch

yo
yarn over

purl
WS: knit stitch

ssk
RS: Slip one stitch as if to knit. Slip another stitch as if to knit. Insert left-hand needle into front of these 2 stitches and knit them together

WAVE MITTENS

by Amanda Lilley

FINISHED MEASUREMENTS

Adult medium to fit 7.5" hand
circumference x 8.5" hand height, plus 6"
cuff, unfolded

YARN

Knit Picks Wool of the Andes Superwash
Bulky (100% Superwash Wool; 137
yards/100g): Mineral Heather 26514, 1
skein

NEEDLES

US 8 (5mm) DPN's, or one size smaller
than needles to obtain gauge
US 9 (5.5mm) DPN's, or size to obtain
gauge

NOTIONS

Yarn Needle
Cable Needle
Waste Yarn
Stitch Marker

GAUGE

16 sts and 20 rows = 4" in cable pattern
on larger needles in the round, blocked

Wave Mittens

Notes:

These cuddly mittens have a distinctive zigzag pattern. Knit in bulky yarn, they work up quickly to keep your hands warm!

K2, P2 Ribbing (worked in the rnd over multiples of 4 sts)
C3R: Place 1 st on CN and hold to back, K2, P1 from CN
C3L: Place 2 sts onto CN and hold to front, P1, K2.

DIRECTIONS
Mittens (make 2)
Cuff
With US 8 needle, loosely CO 32 sts. Join to work in round. PM for beginning of rnd if desired.
Work in K2, P2 Ribbing for 6".

Hand
Switch to US 9 needle
Rnd 1: (P2tog) twice, P1, C3R, *P3, C3R, rep from * to end of rnd. 30 sts.
Rnd 2: P3, K2, *P4, K2, rep from * to last st, P1.
Rnd 3: P2, C3R, *P3, C3R, rep from * to last st, P1.
Rnd 4: P2, *K2, P4, rep from * to last 4 sts, K2, P2.
Rnd 5: P1, *C3R, P3, rep from * to last 5 sts, C3R, P2.
Rnd 6: P1, *K2, P4, rep from * to last 5 sts, K2, P3.
Rnd 7: *C3R, P3, rep from * to end of rnd.
Rnd 8: *K2, P4, rep from * to end of rnd.
Rnd 9: *C3L, P3, rep from * to end of rnd.
Rnd 10: P1, *K2, P4, rep from * to last 5 sts, K2, P3
Rnd 11: P1, *C3L, P3, rep from * to last 5 sts, C3L, P2.
Rnd 12: P2, *K2, P4, rep from * to last 4 sts, K2, P2.
Rnd 13: P2, *C3L, P3, rep from * to last 4 sts, C3L, P1.
Rnd 14: P3, *K2, P4, rep from * to last 3 sts, K2, P1.
Rnd 15: *P3, C3L, rep from * to end of rnd.
Rnd 16, Right Hand: K5 sts with waste yarn. Place these 5 sts

back onto left-hand needle. With working yarn *P4, K2, rep from * to end of rnd.
Rnd 16, Left Hand: *P4, K2, rep from * to last 6 sts, P1, K last 5 sts with waste yarn. Place these 5 sts back onto left-hand needle. With working yarn, P3, K2.
Rnd 17: *P3, C3R, rep from * to end of rnd.
Rnds 18 - 31: Repeat Rnds 2 -15.
Rnd 32: *P4, K2, rep from * to end of rnd.
Rnd 33: Repeat Rnd 17.
Rnd 34 - 39: Repeat Rnds 2 – 7.
Rnd 40: *K2, P2tog, P2, rep from * to end of rnd. 25 sts.
Rnd 41: *C3L, P2tog, rep from * to end of rnd. 20 sts.
Rnd 42: *P1, K1, SSK, rep from * to end of rnd. 15 sts.
Rnd 43: *K2tog, K1, rep from * to end of rnd. 10 sts.
Cut yarn and draw through remaining 10 sts, closing hole.

Thumb
Remove waste yarn and place the 5 sts from the top, and the 5 sts from the bottom, onto DPNs. P1 rnd, picking up 1 st on each side of the base of thumb. 12 sts.
Join in the rnd and purl each rnd until thumb measures 2.5"
*P2tog, rep from * until 3 sts remain on needles. Cut yarn and draw through remaining sts, closing hole.

Finishing
Weave in ends. Wet block mitten into shape.

ZIGZAGGING HAT AND MITTS

by Mone Dräger

FINISHED MEASUREMENTS

The ribbing has a lot of elasticity, so each given size fits circumferences approximately up to an inch smaller or bigger than those given

Hat: S (M, L), circumference 15.25 (17.25, 19.25)" x adjustable 7.5" height

Mittens: S (M, L), circumference: 6.5 (7.75, 9)" x adjustable length from cuff to tip 8.75 (9.25, 9.75)"

YARN

Knit Picks Gloss DK (70% Merino Wool, 30% Silk; 123 yards/50g): Masala 24719 2 (3, 4) balls

NEEDLES

US 6 (4mm) DPNs or two 24" circular needles for two circulars technique, or one 32" or longer circular needle for Magic Loop technique, or size to obtain gauge

NOTIONS

Yarn Needle
Stitch Markers
Scrap yarn or stitch holder

GAUGE

25 sts and 28 rows = 4" in Twisted Rib in the round, blocked

Zigzagging Hat and Mittens

Notes:

Hat and mittens are knit mainly in ribbing for a snug, yet comfortable fit. The decorative element is a zigzagging lace panel, which varies in width and height for hat and mittens. The mittens design is 'un-handed', both mittens are worked the same.

Read all chart rows from right to left, as a RS row.

Eyelet Mock Cable (EMC) (worked over 3 sts)

Pull third st on LH needle over first and second st on LH needle, K1 TBL, YO, K1 TBL.

Make 1 Right (M1R)

With left needle lift strand between last knitted st and first st on the left needle from back to front. K into front of lifted loop.

Make 1 Left (M1L)

With left needle lift strand between last knitted st and first st on the left needle from front to back. K into back of lifted loop.

Twisted Rib (in the round over an even number of sts)

All Rnds: *K1 TBL, P1, rep from * to end of rnd.

DIRECTIONS

Hat

The hat is worked from the brim to the top.

Bottom Edge

Loosely CO 96 (108, 120) sts. Distribute sts across needles as you prefer, PM, and join to work in the round, being careful not to twist.

Work 10 rnds of Twisted Rib.

Lace Section

Work Rnds 1-16 from Zigzag Hat Chart, or follow written instructions below.

Please note that in Rnds 3, 7 and 11, the last EMC of the rnd is completed using the first st of the next rnd.

Rnd 1: *EMC, (P1, K1 TBL) 4 times, P1; rep from * 8 (9, 10) times.

Rnd 2 and all even numbered rnds through Rnd 16: *K1 TBL, P1, rep from * to end of rnd.

Rnd 3: K1 TBL, *P1, EMC, (P1, K1 TBL) twice, P1, EMC; rep from * 8 (9, 10) times; using the first st of the next rnd to complete last EMC.

Rnd 5: *EMC, P1; rep from * to end of rnd.

Rnd 7: K1 TBL, *P1, EMC; rep from * 24 (27, 30) times; using the first st of the next rnd to complete last EMC.

Rnd 9: Rep Rnd 5.

Rnd 11: Rep Rnd 7.

Rnd 13: *(K1 TBL, P1) twice, (EMC, P1) twice; rep from * to end of rnd.

Rnd 15: *(K1 TBL, P1) 3 times, EMC, P1, K1 TBL, P1; rep from to end of rnd.

Hat Body in Ribbing

Work in Twisted Rib for 18 rnds, or until hat measures 2.25" less than desired height.

Crown Shaping

Rnd 1: *SSK, (K1 TBL, P1) 5 times, PM; rep from * to end of rnd. 88 (99, 110) sts.

Rnd 2: *K1 TBL, work as established in ribbing to M, rep from * to end of rnd.

Rnd 3: *SSK, work as established in ribbing to M; rep from * to end of rnd. 80 (90, 100) sts.

Rep Rnds 2-3 five more times. 40 (45, 50) sts.

Rep Rnd 3 four times. 8 (9, 10) sts.

Break yarn and thread through remaining sts. Pull tight to fasten.

Mittens (make 2 the same)

The mittens are worked from the cuff to the top.

Cuff

Loosely CO 40 (48, 56) sts. Distribute sts across needles as you prefer, PM, and join to work in the round, being careful not to twist.

Work in Twisted Rib for 8 rnds.

Lace Section

Work Rnds 1-10 from Zigzag Mittens Chart, or follow written instructions below.

Please note that in Rnds 3 and 7 the last EMC of the rnd is completed using the first st of the next rnd.

Rnd 1: *EMC, (P1, K1 TBL) twice, P1; rep from * 5 (6, 7) times.

Rnd 2 and all even numbered rnds through Rnd 10: *K1 TBL, P1, rep from * to end of rnd.

Rnd 3: K1 TBL, *P1, EMC; rep from * 10 (12, 14) times; using the first st of the next rnd to complete last EMC.

Rnd 5: *EMC, P1; rep from * to end of rnd.

Rnd 7: Rep Rnd 3.

Rnd 9: *(K1 TBL, P1) twice, EMC, P1; rep from to end of rnd.

Mittens Body with Thumb Gusset

Rnd 1: M1L, K1, M1R, PM for Thumb Gusset, *P1, K1 TBL; rep from * to last st, P1. 2 gusset sts inc.

Rnd 2-3: K to M, *P1, K1 TBL; rep from * to last st, P1.

Rnd 4: M1L, K to M, M1R, *P1, K1 TBL; rep from * to last st, P1. 2 gusset sts inc.

Rep Rnds 2-4 four (five, six) more times times, then rep Rnds 2-3 once more. 52 (62, 72) sts.

Divide for Thumb

Place 13 (15, 17) gusset sts on scrap yarn or stitch holder, remove M, CO 3 sts using backward loop method, K to end. 42 (50, 58) sts.

Hand

Rnds 1-4: K3, *P1, K1 TBL; rep from * to last st, P1.

Rnd 5: CDD, *P1, K1 TBL; rep from * to last st, P1. 40 (48, 56) sts.

Work in Twisted Rib for 15 rnds, or until mitten measures 1.75" less than desired length.

Top Shaping

Rnd 1: *SSK, (K1 TBL, P1) 3 times, PM; rep from * to end of rnd. 35 (42, 49) sts.

Rnd 2: *K1 TBL, work as established in ribbing to M, rep from * to end of rnd.

Rnd 3: Rep Rnd 2.

Rnd 4: *SSK, work as established in ribbing to M; rep from * to end of rnd. 30 (36, 42) sts.

Rep Rnds 3-4 two more times. 25 (30, 35) sts.

Rep Rnd 4 four times. 5 (6, 7) sts.

Break yarn and thread through remaining sts. Pull tight to fasten.

Thumb

Starting at the right edge of the gap, with RS facing, PU 2 (3, 4) sts, PM for beginning of the round, return 13 (15, 17) thumb sts from holder onto needle. Distribute sts across needles as you prefer. 15 (18, 21) sts.

Knit for 12 rnds, or until thumb is .5 (.5, .75)" less than desired length.

Decrease Rnd 1: *SSK, K3 (4, 5), PM; rep from * to end. 12 (15, 18) sts.

Decrease Rnd 2: *SSK, K to M; rep from * to end. (9, 12, 15) sts.

Rep Decrease Rnd 2 one (two, three) more times. 6 sts.

Break yarn and thread through remaining sts. Pull tight to fasten.

Finishing

Weave in ends, wash and block lightly.

Zigzag Hat Chart

25	24	23	22	21	20	19	18	17	16	15	14	13	12	11	10	9	8	7	6	5	4	3	2	1	
▨	●	B	●	B	●	B	●	B	●	B	●	B	●	B	●	B	●	B	●	B	●	B	●	B	16
▨	●	B	●	C	○	⌐	●	B	●	B	●	B	●	B	C	○	⌐	●	B	●	B	●	B	●	B	15
▨	●	B	●	B	●	B	●	B	●	B	●	B	●	B	●	B	●	B	●	B	●	B	●	B	14
▨	●	C	○	⌐	●	C	○	⌐	●	B	●	C	○	⌐	●	C	○	⌐	●	B	●	B	●	B	13
▨	●	B	●	B	●	B	●	B	●	B	●	B	●	B	●	B	●	B	●	B	●	B	●	▨	12
C	○	⌐	●	C	○	⌐	●	C	○	⌐	●	C	○	⌐	●	C	○	⌐	●	C	○	⌐	●	B	11
▨	●	B	●	B	●	B	●	B	●	B	●	B	●	B	●	B	●	B	●	B	●	B	●	B	10
▨	●	C	○	⌐	●	C	○	⌐	●	C	○	⌐	●	C	○	⌐	●	C	○	⌐	●	C	○	⌐	9
▨	●	B	●	B	●	B	●	B	●	B	●	B	●	B	●	B	●	B	●	B	●	B	●	▨	8
C	○	⌐	●	C	○	⌐	●	C	○	⌐	●	C	○	⌐	●	C	○	⌐	●	C	○	⌐	●	B	7
▨	●	B	●	B	●	B	●	B	●	B	●	B	●	B	●	B	●	B	●	B	●	B	●	B	6
▨	●	C	○	⌐	●	C	○	⌐	●	C	○	⌐	●	C	○	⌐	●	C	○	⌐	●	C	○	⌐	5
▨	●	B	●	B	●	B	●	B	●	B	●	B	●	B	●	B	●	B	●	B	●	B	●	▨	4
C	○	⌐	●	B	●	B	●	C	○	⌐	●	C	○	⌐	●	B	●	B	●	C	○	⌐	●	B	3
▨	●	B	●	B	●	B	●	B	●	B	●	B	●	B	●	B	●	B	●	B	●	B	●	B	2
▨	●	B	●	B	●	B	●	B	●	C	○	⌐	●	B	●	B	●	B	●	B	●	C	○	⌐	1

Legend

Eyelet Mock Cable — Pull third st on LH needle over first and second st on LH needle, K1 TBL, YO, K1 TBL.

● **purl** — purl stitch

B **knit tbl** — Knit stitch through back loop

▨ **No Stitch** — Placeholder - No stitch made.

☐ **pattern repeat**

Zigzag Mittens Chart

17	16	15	14	13	12	11	10	9	8	7	6	5	4	3	2	1	
▨	●	B	●	B	●	B	●	B	●	B	●	B	●	B	●	B	10
▨	●	C	○	⌐	●	B	●	B	●	C	○	⌐	●	B	●	B	9
▨	●	B	●	B	●	B	●	B	●	B	●	B	●	B	●	▨	8
C	○	⌐	●	C	○	⌐	●	C	○	⌐	●	C	○	⌐	●	B	7
▨	●	B	●	B	●	B	●	B	●	B	●	B	●	B	●	B	6
▨	●	C	○	⌐	●	C	○	⌐	●	C	○	⌐	●	C	○	⌐	5
▨	●	B	●	B	●	B	●	B	●	B	●	B	●	B	●	▨	4
C	○	⌐	●	C	○	⌐	●	C	○	⌐	●	C	○	⌐	●	B	3
▨	●	B	●	B	●	B	●	B	●	B	●	B	●	B	●	B	2
▨	●	B	●	B	●	C	○	⌐	●	B	●	B	●	C	○	⌐	1

ARRI HAT

by Zabet Kempfert

FINISHED MEASUREMENTS

19.25 (21.25, 23.5)" circumference x 9.5"
high, not including pom-pom

YARN

Knit Picks Biggo (50% Superwash Merino
Wool, 50% Nylon): MC Cobblestone
Heather 26087, C1 Bare 26089, 1 hank
each

NEEDLES

US 10.5 (6.5mm) 16" circular needles plus
DPN's, or size to obtain gauge

NOTIONS

Yarn Needle
Stitch Markers
Pompom Maker (optional)

GAUGE

15 sts and 17 rows = 4" in stranded St st in
the round, blocked

Arri Hat

Notes:

The Arri Hat features an easy colorwork pattern that knits up quickly due to the bulky yarn used. Feel free to knit the brim in C1 instead of MC if you want to incorporate more of your contrasting yarn color. Because this hat is worked in the round, read each row of the chart from right to left.

Yarn dominance is a factor in this pattern. C1 is intended to be the dominant color in the colorwork sections. If you knit colorwork with one yarn in each hand, C1 should be held in your left hand and MC in your right. If you hold both yarns in one hand, keep C1 to the left of MC. Whichever way you prefer to knit colorwork patterns, remember that, when looking at a single row of colorwork stiches, the dominant yarn floats should sit below the background yarn floats.

K2, P2 Ribbing (worked in the rnd over multiples of 4 sts)
All Rnds: *K2, P2; rep from * to end of rnd.

DIRECTIONS
Hat
Loosely CO 72 (80, 88) sts in MC. PM and join to work in the round, being careful not to twist sts.
Work in K2, P2 Ribbing for 2".
Knit 1 round in MC.
Join C1 and begin working from Arri Chart, repeating the 4 st pattern 18 (20, 22) times around the hat and reading each chart row from right to left, knitting all sts. Work Rounds 1-15 once. Break C1.
Knit even in MC until piece measures 6" from CO edge, or 3.5" less than desired height.

Decreases
Switch to DPNs when necessary.
Decrease Round 1: *K6, K2tog; rep from * around 9 (10, 11) times. 63 (70, 77) sts.
K 2 rnds even.
Decrease Round 2: *K5, K2tog; rep from * around 9 (10, 11) times. 54 (60, 66) sts.
K 2 rnds even.
Decrease Round 3: *K4, K2tog; rep from * around 9 (10, 11) times. 45 (50, 55) sts.
K 1 rnd even.
Decrease Round 4: *K3, K2tog; rep from * around 9 (10, 11) times. 36 (40, 44) sts.
K 1 rnd even.
Decrease Round 5: *K2, K2tog; rep from * around 9 (10, 11) times. 27 (30, 33) sts.
K 1 rnd even.
Decrease Round 6: *K1, K2tog; rep from * around 9 (10, 11) times. 18 (20, 22) sts.
K 1 rnd even.
K2tog around 9 (10, 11) times. 9 (10, 11) sts.

Break MC. Draw yarn end through remaining live sts. Pull tight to close. Make a pompom with C1 and attach to top of hat.

Finishing
Weave in ends, wash, and block to finished measurements.

Arri Chart

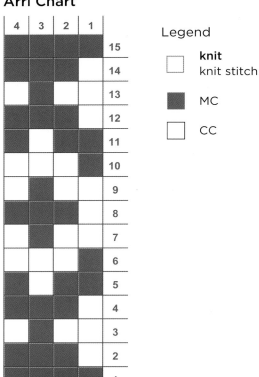

Legend

☐ **knit** knit stitch

◼ MC

☐ CC

Abbreviations		M	marker		stitch	TBL	through back loop
BO	bind off	M1	make one stitch	RH	right hand	TFL	through front loop
cn	cable needle	M1L	make one left-leaning	rnd(s)	round(s)	tog	together
CC	contrast color		stitch	RS	right side	W&T	wrap & turn (see
CDD	Centered double dec	M1R	make one right-lean-	Sk	skip		specific instructions
CO	cast on		ing stitch	Sk2p	sl 1, k2tog, pass		in pattern)
cont	continue	MC	main color		slipped stitch over	WE	work even
dec	decrease(es)	P	purl		k2tog: 2 sts dec	WS	wrong side
DPN(s)	double pointed	P2tog	purl 2 sts together	SKP	sl, k, psso: 1 st dec	WYIB	with yarn in back
	needle(s)	PM	place marker	SL	slip	WYIF	with yarn in front
EOR	every other row	PFB	purl into the front and	SM	slip marker	YO	yarn over
inc	increase		back of stitch	SSK	sl, sl, k these 2 sts tog		
K	knit	PSSO	pass slipped stitch	SSP	sl, sl, p these 2 sts tog		
K2tog	knit two sts together		over		tbl		
KFB	knit into the front and	PU	pick up	SSSK	sl, sl, sl, k these 3 sts		
	back of stitch	P-wise	purlwise		tog		
K-wise	knitwise	rep	repeat	St st	stockinette stitch		
LH	left hand	Rev St st	reverse stockinette	sts	stitch(es)		

Knit Picks ®

Knit Picks yarn is both luxe and affordable—a seeming contradiction trounced! But it's not just about the pretty colors; we also care deeply about fiber quality and fair labor practices, leaving you with a gorgeously reliable product you'll turn to time and time again.

THIS COLLECTION FEATURES

Palette
Fingering Weight
100% Peruvian Highland Wool

Stroll
Fingering Weight
75% Superwash Merino Wool,
25% Nylon

Biggo
Bulky Weight
50% Superwash Merino Wool
50% Nylon

Swish DK
DK Weight
100% Superwash Merino Wool

Preciosa Tonal Worsted
Worsted Weight
100% Merino Wool

Wool of the Andes Worsted
Worsted Weight
100% Peruvian Highland Wool

Swish Worsted
Worsted Weight
100% Superwash Merino Wool

Brava Bulky
Bulky Weight
100% Premium Acrylic

Gloss Fingering
Fingering Weight
70% Merino Wool, 30% Silk

Diadem Solid DK
DK Weight
50% Baby Alpaca, 50% Mulberry Silk

Tuff Puff
Super Bulky Weight
100% Wool

City Tweed HW/Arar
Aran Weight
55% Merino Wool, 25% Superfine Alpa
20% Donegal Tweed

Hawthorne Fingering
80% Superwash Fine Highland
Wool, 20% Polyamide (Nylon)

Wool of the Andes Superwash Worsted
Worsted Weight
100% Superwash Wool

Wool of the Andes Superwash Bulky
Bulky Weight
100% Superwash Wool

Gloss DK
DK Weight
70% Merino Wool, 30% Silk